Top 75 Yummy Mexican Recipes

(Top 75 Yummy Mexican Recipes - Volume 1)

Paula Lopez

Copyright: Published in the United States by Paula Lopez/ © PAULA LOPEZ

Published on August, 29 2020

All rights reserved. No part of this publication may be reproduced, stored in retrieval system, copied in any form or by any means, electronic, mechanical, photocopying, recording or otherwise transmitted without written permission from the publisher. Please do not participate in or encourage piracy of this material in any way. You must not circulate this book in any format. PAULA LOPEZ does not control or direct users' actions and is not responsible for the information or content shared, harm and/or actions of the book readers.

In accordance with the U.S. Copyright Act of 1976, the scanning, uploading and electronic sharing of any part of this book without the permission of the publisher constitute unlawful piracy and theft of the author's intellectual property. If you would like to use material from the book (other than just simply for reviewing the book), prior permission must be obtained by contacting the author at author@bunrecipes.com

Thank you for your support of the author's rights.

Content

75 AWESOME MEXICAN RECIPES 4

1. 1 Dish Taco Bake 4
2. Adobo Herb Salsa 4
3. Amazing Mexican Quinoa Salad 5
4. Amy's Cilantro Cream Sauce 5
5. Amy's Spicy Beans And Rice 6
6. Authentic Mexican Restaurant Style Salsa .. 6
7. Bab's South Of The Border Taco Dip 6
8. Baked Beef Chiles Rellenos Casserole 7
9. Beer Braised Chicken Tacos 8
10. Breakfast Burrito Bites 8
11. Chicken Cheddar And Guacamole Burgers 9
12. Chicken Pineapple Fajitas 9
13. Chicken Suiza Cornbread Bake 10
14. Chicken Taco Filling 10
15. Chicken And Vegetable Quesadillas 11
16. Coconut Margarita 11
17. Easy Chicken Fajita Soup 12
18. Easy Tortilla Soup 12
19. Elotes (Mexican Corn In A Cup) 13
20. Fall In Love (with) Guacamole 13
21. Fiesta Guacamole 13
22. Fresh Tomato Salsa Restaurant Style 14
23. Fruit Salsa 14
24. Gravel Salad 15
25. Healthier Slow Cooker Chicken Tortilla Soup 15
26. Italian Nachos Restaurant Style 16
27. Jalapeno Cream Cheese Chicken Enchiladas 16
28. Jicama Mango Slaw 17
29. Jicama Salad With Cilantro And Lime 17
30. Jim's Pork Chorizo 18
31. Jimmy Dean 6 Layer Breakfast Casserole . 18
32. Jimmy's Mexican Pizza 18
33. Ken's Kickin' Posole 19
34. Margarita Con Cerveza 20
35. Marinated Flank Steak 20
36. Menudo 21
37. Mexi Hominy 21
38. Mexican Chicken Crepes 21
39. Mexican Corn Bread Casserole 22
40. Mexican Mole Sauce 23
41. Mexican Pot Roast 23
42. Mexican Taco Quinoa Bowl With Chicken 24
43. Mexican Vegetable Rice Bowl 24
44. Mexican Zucchini Cheese Soup 25
45. Mommy's Lemonade (Margaritas) 25
46. My Ultimate Guacamole 26
47. Nacho Tacos 26
48. Peanut Butter Banana Quesadilla 26
49. Pie Iron Tacos 27
50. Pollo Con Nopales (Chicken And Cactus) 27
51. Prickly Pear Cactus Margarita 28
52. Quesadillas De Los Bajos 28
53. Quick And Easy Taco Dip 29
54. Red Pepper Chicken 29
55. Red Ribbon Roasted Salsa 30
56. Restaurant Style Cheesy Poblano Pepper Soup 31
57. Restaurant Style Tequila Lime Chicken 31
58. Rompope (Mexican Eggnog) 32
59. Shiner® Bock Shredded Chicken Tacos ... 33
60. Shrimp And Jalapeno Nachos 33
61. Shrimp And Octopus Soup (Caldo De Camaron Y Pulpo) 34
62. Shrimp, Jicama And Chile Vinegar Salad .. 34
63. Simple Shrimp Tostadas 35
64. Slow Cooker Cilantro Lime Chicken 35
65. Slow Cooker Spicy Chicken 36
66. Southwest Corn Chowder 36
67. Southwestern Chicken Pitas With Chipotle Sauce 37
68. Spicy Cheesy Refried Beans 37
69. Sylvia's Pork Tamales 38
70. Taco Slaw 39
71. Tongue Tacos 39
72. Traditional Mexican Guacamole 40
73. Traditional Mexican Street Tacos 40
74. Vegan Mexican Quinoa Bowl With Green Chile Cilantro Sauce 40
75. Vegetarian Tortilla Soup With Avocado ... 41

INDEX 42

CONCLUSION 44

75 Awesome Mexican Recipes

***

1. 1 Dish Taco Bake

Serving: 6 | Prep: 20mins | Ready in:

Ingredients

- Taco Meat Filling:
- 1 pound ground beef
- 1 (1.25 ounce) package taco seasoning
- Batter:
- Mazola Pure® Cooking Spray
- 3/4 cup all-purpose flour
- 1/2 cup masa corn flour OR corn meal
- 2 envelopes Fleischmann's® RapidRise Yeast
- 1 tablespoon sugar
- 1/2 teaspoon salt
- 3/4 cup very warm milk (120 degrees F to 130 degrees F)
- 3 tablespoons Mazola® Corn Oil
- 1 egg
- Topping:
- 1 cup chunky salsa
- 1 cup shredded Mexican-style cheese
- 1 cup corn chips, partially crushed

Direction

- Brown the ground beef and drain. Put in the taco seasoning and stir them well.
- Combine the batter ingredients in the pre-sprayed 9.5-in. deep pie dish.
- Add the taco meat filling on top of the batter. Distribute the salsa equally on the meat; drizzle with the corn chips and shredded cheese.
- Bake by putting into the COLD oven; set the temperature to 350°F. Bake till done, about half an hour.

Nutrition Information

- Calories: 526 calories;
- Sodium: 1223
- Total Carbohydrate: 41.7
- Cholesterol: 101
- Protein: 23.6
- Total Fat: 29.4

2. Adobo Herb Salsa

Serving: 4 | Prep: 15mins | Ready in:

Ingredients

- 1 (28 ounce) can diced tomatoes
- 1 green bell pepper, diced
- 1/4 cup minced red onion
- 1/4 cup minced fresh cilantro
- 1 tablespoon adobo sauce from canned chipotle peppers
- 1 tablespoon chopped fresh tarragon
- 1/2 teaspoon salt
- 2 tablespoons balsamic vinegar

Direction

- Toss together vinegar, tarragon, adobo sauce, cilantro, onion, bell pepper and tomatoes in a bowl, then season with salt to taste. Cover and chill for a minimum of a half hour.

Nutrition Information

- Calories: 59 calories;
- Cholesterol: 0
- Protein: 2.1
- Total Fat: 0.2

- Sodium: 621
- Total Carbohydrate: 10.4

3. Amazing Mexican Quinoa Salad

Serving: 8 | Prep: 20mins | Ready in:

Ingredients

- 2 cups cooked quinoa
- 1 (15 ounce) can pinto beans, rinsed and drained
- 1 (15 ounce) can kidney beans, rinsed and drained
- 1 (14 ounce) can corn
- 1 red onion, chopped
- 1 cup cooked brown rice
- 1 red bell pepper, chopped
- 1/4 cup chopped fresh cilantro
- Dressing:
- 3/4 cup olive oil
- 1/3 cup red wine vinegar
- 1 tablespoon chili powder, or to taste
- 2 cloves garlic, mashed
- 1/2 teaspoon salt
- 1/2 teaspoon ground black pepper
- 1/4 teaspoon cayenne pepper, or to taste

Direction

- In a plastic container or a glass with lid, combine the cilantro, red bell pepper, brown rice, red onion, corn, kidney beans, pinto beans and quinoa.
- In a bowl, mix together the cayenne pepper, black pepper, salt, garlic, chili powder, vinegar and olive oil; then place over quinoa mixture and coat by tossing. Then, cover the bowl with a lid and place inside the refrigerator for at least 2 hours until flavors are enhanced.
- Mix again before serving.

Nutrition Information

- Calories: 397 calories;
- Total Fat: 22.6
- Sodium: 532
- Total Carbohydrate: 42.4
- Cholesterol: 0
- Protein: 9.1

4. Amy's Cilantro Cream Sauce

Serving: 4 | Prep: 10mins | Ready in:

Ingredients

- 1 (8 ounce) package cream cheese, softened
- 1 tablespoon sour cream
- 1 (7 ounce) can tomatillo salsa
- 1 teaspoon freshly ground black pepper
- 1 teaspoon celery salt
- 1/2 teaspoon ground cumin
- 2 teaspoons garlic powder
- 1 bunch fresh cilantro, chopped
- 1 tablespoon fresh lime juice

Direction

- In a food processor or blender, combine lime juice, cilantro, garlic powder, cumin, celery salt, pepper, salsa, sour cream and cream cheese. Blend until they become creamy and smooth. Transfer to a serving bowl.

Nutrition Information

- Calories: 230 calories;
- Protein: 5
- Total Fat: 20.5
- Sodium: 868
- Total Carbohydrate: 7.1
- Cholesterol: 63

5. Amy's Spicy Beans And Rice

Serving: 6 | Prep: 5mins | Ready in:

Ingredients

- 1 1/2 cups water
- 1/2 cup uncooked brown rice
- 2 (15 ounce) cans black beans, undrained
- 2 fresh jalapeno peppers, seeded and chopped
- 1 teaspoon ground cumin, or to taste
- 1 tablespoon chili powder, or to taste
- black pepper to taste
- 1/2 cup shredded sharp Cheddar cheese
- 2 fresh green onions, chopped
- 1/2 (2 ounce) can sliced black olives, drained

Direction

- Preheat the oven to 175 °C or 350 °F.
- Boil water in a saucepan. Put in the rice and mix. Lower the heat, put a cover on and let simmer for 40 minutes.
- In the meantime, put the beans into a 2-quart casserole. Scatter black pepper, chili powder, cumin and jalapenos over.
- In the prepped oven, bake for half an hour. Scatter olives, green onions and cheese on top. Bake for an additional 5 to 10 minutes.
- Top cooked rice with beans and serve.

Nutrition Information

- Calories: 96 calories;
- Total Carbohydrate: 11.2
- Cholesterol: 10
- Protein: 3.7
- Total Fat: 4.3
- Sodium: 114

6. Authentic Mexican Restaurant Style Salsa

Serving: 14 | Prep: 5mins | Ready in:

Ingredients

- 1 (28 ounce) can crushed tomatoes
- 10 slices pickled jalapeno peppers with juice, or to taste
- 10 cilantro leaves
- 1/2 teaspoon salt
- 1/4 teaspoon garlic powder

Direction

- In a blender, process garlic powder, salt, cilantro leaves, juice, jalapeno peppers and crushed tomatoes until smooth. Chill for about 8 hours or overnight.

Nutrition Information

- Calories: 19 calories;
- Sodium: 205
- Total Carbohydrate: 4.3
- Cholesterol: 0
- Protein: 1
- Total Fat: 0.2

7. Bab's South Of The Border Taco Dip

Serving: 20 | Prep: 30mins | Ready in:

Ingredients

- 1 pound ground beef
- 2 cloves garlic, minced
- 2 chipotle peppers in adobo sauce, minced
- 1/2 teaspoon ground cumin
- 1/2 teaspoon chili powder
- 2 (8 ounce) packages cream cheese, softened
- 1 red bell pepper, diced
- 2 teaspoons lime juice, or as needed
- 1 cup chopped fresh tomato
- 1 (6 ounce) can sliced black olives, drained
- 2 cups shredded Cheddar cheese
- 2 cups chopped iceberg lettuce, divided

- 1/2 cup chopped green onion
- 1 (16 ounce) jar taco sauce
- 2 avocados - peeled, pitted, and diced
- 2 lime, zested and juiced
- 1/2 cup sour cream
- 1/2 cup chopped fresh cilantro

Direction

- In a large skillet over medium heat, cook ground beef for about 10 minutes or until crumbly and browned. Drain excess grease.
- Stir in chili powder, cumin, chipotle pepper, and garlic; cook for about 5 minutes or just until flavors blend. Put to one side and allow to cool.
- Combine cream cheese with 2 teaspoons lime juice and red bell pepper in a bowl to achieve a spreadable mixture. Spread cream cheese mixture over the bottom of a 9x13-inch baking dish or large springform pan.
- Layer cooled beef mixture atop cream cheese.
- Arrange layers of tomatoes, black olives, Cheddar cheese, half the lettuce, green onion, the rest of lettuce, and taco sauce over beef.
- Lightly combine avocado with zest and juice of 2 limes. Spread avocado mixtures over the taco sauce.
- Dot dollops of sour cream atop mixture of the dish and scatter with cilantro to finish the dip.

Nutrition Information

- Calories: 234 calories;
- Protein: 9.3
- Total Fat: 19.4
- Sodium: 376
- Total Carbohydrate: 6.5
- Cholesterol: 53

8. Baked Beef Chiles Rellenos Casserole

Serving: 10 | Prep: 20mins | Ready in:

Ingredients

- 6 large poblano peppers, halved and seeded
- 1 1/2 pounds ground beef, or to taste
- 1 tablespoon chili powder
- 2 cloves garlic, minced
- 1 teaspoon ground cumin
- 1 teaspoon dried oregano
- 1/4 teaspoon ground cayenne pepper
- 1/4 teaspoon ground paprika
- 1/4 teaspoon ground dried chipotle pepper
- salt and ground black pepper to taste
- 1 large onion, chopped
- 2 (14.5 ounce) cans diced tomatoes with green chile peppers
- cooking spray
- 3 cups shredded Mexican cheese blend, or to taste

Direction

- Place oven rack 6 inches from the source of heat then preheat the broiler. Place aluminum foil on baking sheet. Put the poblano peppers on the baking sheet with the cut facing down.
- Let the poblano chile peppers cook under broiler for 5-8 minutes until skins turn black and blistered. Put the cooked peppers in a bowl then seal it with plastic wrap tightly. Let the peppers steam for 10 minutes as they cool down.
- Heat a big frying pan on medium high heat. Add in the chili powder, beef, cumin, garlic, cayenne pepper, oregano, chipotle pepper, paprika, black pepper and salt. Let it cook while stirring until the pinkish color of the beef goes away, 4 minutes. Mix in the onion and cook for 2 minutes until slightly tender. Add in the tomatoes with the green chiles. Cook for another 5 minutes until onions become translucent. Set aside to cool.
- Heat the oven to 350°F or 175°C. Apply cooking spray to the casserole dish.
- Remove burnt skins of the poblano peppers with cool running water. Dry the peppers with paper towels. Put a layer of the peppers on bottom of the dish then put about 1/3 of beef

- mixture on top. Cover the mixture with a cup of shredded Mexican cheese blend. Repeat the process for two more layers.
- Let it bake in the oven, without cover, for about 35 minutes until the top becomes golden brown.

Nutrition Information

- Calories: 325 calories;
- Total Fat: 23.3
- Sodium: 695
- Total Carbohydrate: 8.9
- Cholesterol: 80
- Protein: 21.5

9. Beer Braised Chicken Tacos

Serving: 8 | Prep: 15mins | Ready in:

Ingredients

- Sauce:
- 2 tablespoons vegetable oil
- 1 large onion, finely chopped
- 2 cups shredded cooked chicken
- 3/4 cup Mexican beer
- 1 tablespoon ground ancho chiles
- 1/2 teaspoon ground cumin
- 1/2 teaspoon salt
- 1 (10 ounce) can Old El Paso® green or mild red enchilada sauce
- Tacos:
- 8 Old El Paso® taco shells, heated as directed on box
- 1 (4 ounce) can Old El Paso® chopped green chiles
- 1/2 cup sour cream
- 1/2 cup chopped fresh cilantro
- 8 lime wedges

Direction

- Heat the oil in 12 inches skillet on moderately-high heat. Put in chicken and onion; cook for a minute or till onion is soft. Mix in the rest of the sauce ingredients. Heat till boiling. Lower the heat to low; cook for 20 minutes with no cover, mixing from time to time.
- Into the taco shells, scoop the chicken mixture; put the rest of the ingredients on top.

Nutrition Information

- Calories: 189 calories;
- Total Carbohydrate: 13.4
- Cholesterol: 16
- Protein: 5.5
- Total Fat: 12.1
- Sodium: 455

10. Breakfast Burrito Bites

Serving: 4 | Prep: | Ready in:

Ingredients

- 1 (12 ounce) package Johnsonville® Original, Brown Sugar Honey, or Vermont Maple Syrup Breakfast Sausage links
- 4 (6 inch) Mission® Super Soft Flour Tortillas
- 1/4 cup shredded sharp Cheddar cheese
- 3 tablespoons red pepper jelly
- 2 tablespoons sliced green onions

Direction

- Preheat an oven to 350°F.
- Put sausage in a square 8-inch nonstick baking pan. Follow package directions to bake sausage.
- Take sausage from baking pan; put aside.
- Cut tortillas to 4 equal quarters; use plastic wrap to cover.
- On a work surface, put 1 tortilla wedge. On the wide end of wedges, put 1 sausage link.

- Brush water on pointed tortilla end. Roll up; press to seal. Put, seam side down, in pan.
- Repeat with leftover sausage links.
- Bake it for 5 minutes.
- Flip seam side up; sprinkle cheese. Bake till cheese melts for 3 minutes. Slightly cool.
- Top with green onions and red pepper jelly.

Nutrition Information

- Calories: 446 calories;
- Total Carbohydrate: 29.4
- Cholesterol: 62
- Protein: 21.8
- Total Fat: 26.5
- Sodium: 1282

11. Chicken Cheddar And Guacamole Burgers

Serving: 4 | Prep: 15mins | Ready in:

Ingredients

- 1 1/2 pounds ground chicken
- 1/2 cup minced yellow onion
- 1/3 cup minced fresh cilantro
- 1/3 cup shredded Cheddar cheese
- 2 cloves garlic, minced
- 1 jalapeno pepper, seeded and minced
- 1/2 lime, juiced
- 1 teaspoon ground cumin
- 1 teaspoon paprika
- 1/2 teaspoon Kosher salt
- 1/2 teaspoon ground black pepper
- 4 slices Cheddar cheese
- 4 hamburger buns, split and toasted
- 1/4 cup guacamole, or to taste
- 4 teaspoons chopped fresh cilantro, or to taste

Direction

- Preheat the outdoor grill for medium-high heat and grease grate lightly with oil.
- In a bowl, combine pepper, salt, paprika, cumin, lime juice, jalapeno pepper, garlic, Cheddar cheese, 1/3 cup cilantro and ground chicken; form into 4 patties.
- On the grill, cook patties for 3 to 4 minutes till the bottom is browned; turn the burgers and put 1 slice of Cheddar cheese on top. Keep cooking for 1 to 2 minutes longer till not pink in the middle anymore. An inserted instant-read thermometer into the middle should register 70 °C or 160 °F. Move burgers to a plate, allow to rest for 3 minutes till juices are reabsorbed into the meat.
- On split buns, place the burgers and put cilantro and guacamole on top.

Nutrition Information

- Calories: 523 calories;
- Total Fat: 21.9
- Sodium: 811
- Total Carbohydrate: 27.6
- Cholesterol: 143
- Protein: 52.1

12. Chicken Pineapple Fajitas

Serving: 4 | Prep: 15mins | Ready in:

Ingredients

- 8 (6 inch) flour tortillas
- 1 pound skinless, boneless chicken breast halves - cut into strips
- 2 small red bell peppers, cut into strips
- 2 teaspoons Jamaican jerk seasoning
- 1/8 teaspoon ground black pepper
- 4 slices canned pineapple, chopped
- 1 tablespoon vegetable oil
- chopped fresh cilantro
- lime wedges

Direction

- Set oven to 175°C (or 350°F) and begin preheating. Cover tortillas with aluminum foil; heat in the oven.
- In a large bowl, mix together pepper, jerk seasoning, bell pepper and chicken, then put aside. Bring a large skillet to medium-high heat, then grease with cooking spray. Put in pineapple and cook for about 4-6 minutes until browned. Take pineapple out of the pan and put aside.
- Set skillet back to the stove, stream in vegetable oil and start heating. Put in peppers and chicken; cook, stirring, chicken for about 6 minutes until no pink meat remains. Stir cooked pineapple into the mixture. Place onto the warmed tortillas, decorate with cilantro and a squeeze of lime, then serve.

Nutrition Information

- Calories: 410 calories;
- Total Fat: 10
- Sodium: 709
- Total Carbohydrate: 46.3
- Cholesterol: 66
- Protein: 32.2

13. Chicken Suiza Cornbread Bake

Serving: 12 | Prep: 20mins | Ready in:

Ingredients

- Cornbread Crust:
- 1/2 cup butter
- 1 onion, finely chopped
- 1 clove garlic, minced
- 1 (15.25 ounce) can whole kernel corn, drained
- 1 (15 ounce) can cream-style corn, drained
- 1/4 teaspoon salt
- 1/2 cup egg substitute
- 1 (8.5 ounce) package corn bread mix
- Chicken Topping:
- 2 1/3 cups chopped cooked chicken breast
- 2 tablespoons canned green chile peppers, chopped
- 4 ounces sliced fresh mushrooms
- 1 1/2 cups reduced-fat sour cream
- 1/4 teaspoon salt, or to taste
- 1/4 teaspoon ground black pepper, or to taste
- 1 (8 ounce) package Monterey Jack cheese, shredded

Direction

- Set an oven to 190°C (375°F) and start preheating. Coat a 9x13-inch baking dish with cooking spray.
- In a small skillet, melt the butter on medium heat. Add garlic and onion; cook for 4-6 minutes while mixing until tender. Take off the heat, then put aside. Mix the egg substitute, salt, cream-style corn and corn in a large bowl. Whisk in the muffin mix. Then fold in the cooked onion mixture. Pour into the greased baking dish.
- Mix pepper, salt, sour cream, mushrooms, green chiles and chicken in a large bowl. Scoop on top of the corn mixture to within 1 inch from the edge. Scatter cheese over the top.
- In the prepared oven, bake until the edges turn golden brown, or for 35-40 minutes.

Nutrition Information

- Calories: 378 calories;
- Total Fat: 21.8
- Sodium: 857
- Total Carbohydrate: 30.1
- Cholesterol: 70
- Protein: 17.9

14. Chicken Taco Filling

Serving: 4 | Prep: 5mins | Ready in:

Ingredients

- 1 (1.25 ounce) package dry taco seasoning mix
- 1 cup chicken broth
- 1 pound skinless, boneless chicken breasts

Direction

- Mix together taco seasoning and chicken broth in a bowl.
- Put the chicken breasts into a slow cooker and pour over the chicken with the chicken broth mixture.
- Put the lid on to cover and cook on Low setting for around 6-8 hours.
- To serve, shred the chicken.

Nutrition Information

- Calories: 149 calories;
- Cholesterol: 60
- Protein: 22.3
- Total Fat: 2.4
- Sodium: 935
- Total Carbohydrate: 6.3

15. Chicken And Vegetable Quesadillas

Serving: 2 | Prep: 25mins | Ready in:

Ingredients

- 1 tablespoon olive oil
- 2 cloves garlic, minced, or more to taste
- 1/2 yellow squash, cut into 1/2-inch cubes
- 3/4 cup diced rotisserie chicken meat
- 1/2 red bell pepper, cut into 1/2-inch squares
- salt to taste
- olive oil cooking spray
- 4 whole wheat tortillas
- sharp Cheddar cheese (optional)
- 1/2 cup rinsed and drained canned black beans
- 1/2 avocado, mashed
- 1 tablespoon chopped fresh cilantro

Direction

- Heat 1 tbsp. of the olive oil on medium-high heat in the skillet. Sauté the garlic in the hot oil for roughly 60 seconds or till becoming fragrant. Put in the yellow squash; cook and whisk for 1-2 minutes or till becoming tender a bit. Whisk the bell pepper and chicken to the squash mixture; cook and whisk for roughly 2 minutes longer or till thoroughly heated. Use the salt to season the chicken mixture and move into the bowl.
- Spray a tortilla with the olive oil cooking spray and add into hot skillet. Add 1 slice of Cheddar cheese on tortilla and spread half of chicken-vegetable mixture over the top. Scoop half of black beans on the chicken-vegetable mixture and half of avocado on black beans. Drizzle half of cilantro on avocado. Use the cooking spray to spray another tortilla and add on the top. Keep cooking for 2-3 minutes or till the tortilla's bottom turns crisp; lightly turn the quesadilla over and cook for roughly 4 minutes longer or till the tortilla's bottom turns crisp and the cheese melts. Repeat the process with the rest ingredients to have the second quesadilla.

Nutrition Information

- Calories: 641 calories;
- Total Fat: 31.8
- Sodium: 899
- Total Carbohydrate: 71.9
- Cholesterol: 71
- Protein: 33.3

16. Coconut Margarita

Serving: 8 | Prep: 10mins | Ready in:

Ingredients

- 2 cups sweet and sour mix (such as Bone Daddy®)
- 1 cup tequila (such as Cuervo Gold®)
- 1/2 cup triple sec liqueur
- 1/2 cup coconut milk
- 2 limes, juiced

Direction

- In a pitcher, vigorously stir the coconut milk, sweet and sour mix, lime juice, tequila and triple sec together to blend. Pour the cocktail mix over ice and serve.

Nutrition Information

- Calories: 272 calories;
- Total Fat: 3.1
- Sodium: 3
- Total Carbohydrate: 32.2
- Cholesterol: 0
- Protein: 0.3

17. Easy Chicken Fajita Soup

Serving: 10 | Prep: 20mins | Ready in:

Ingredients

- 2 tablespoons vegetable oil
- 1 pound skinless, boneless chicken breasts, cut into strips
- 1 (1.27 ounce) packet fajita seasoning
- 1 red bell pepper, cut into thin strips
- 1 green bell pepper, cut into thin strips
- 1 poblano pepper, cut into thin strips
- 1 large onion, cut into thin strips
- 1 (14.5 ounce) can fire roasted diced tomatoes
- 1 (15 ounce) can seasoned black beans
- 1 (14 ounce) can chicken broth
- 1 dash hot sauce
- salt and pepper to taste

Direction

- In a big soup pot, heat oil over medium heat. Add chicken to the hot oil, cook for 10 minutes until turning brown, mixing sometimes. Sprinkle over the browned chicken with fajita seasoning and mix thoroughly to blend. Add onion, poblano pepper, green and red bell pepper to the seasoned chicken. Stir and cook over medium heat for 10 minutes until the vegetables are tender.
- Add chicken broth, black beans, and the fire-roasted tomatoes to the vegetables and chicken in the pot. Boil the soup over high heat, and then lower the heat to medium-low, and simmer without a cover for 30 minutes, mixing sometimes.
- Use pepper, salt, and hot sauce to season the soup and then enjoy.

Nutrition Information

- Calories: 143 calories;
- Cholesterol: 24
- Protein: 12.4
- Total Fat: 5.5
- Sodium: 714
- Total Carbohydrate: 15.6

18. Easy Tortilla Soup

Serving: 2 | Prep: | Ready in:

Ingredients

- 2 (10.5 ounce) cans condensed chicken and rice soup
- 1 (10 ounce) can diced tomatoes with green chile peppers
- 1 (8 ounce) can tomato sauce
- 8 ounces tortilla chips
- 4 ounces shredded Cheddar cheese

Direction

- In a medium-sized saucepan, mix tomato sauce, tomatoes and chilies, and soup together over medium-high heat. Barely boil and take away from heat. On the bottom of a separate bowl, put some tortilla chips and sprinkle over the chips with cheese. Add the soup to the cheese and chips.

Nutrition Information

- Calories: 977 calories;
- Cholesterol: 74
- Protein: 34
- Total Fat: 50.2
- Sodium: 3960
- Total Carbohydrate: 103.6

19. Elotes (Mexican Corn In A Cup)

Serving: 4 | Prep: 10mins | Ready in:

Ingredients

- 2 (15.5 ounce) cans whole kernel corn, drained
- 4 tablespoons mayonnaise, or to taste
- 4 tablespoons grated Parmesan cheese, or to taste
- 4 teaspoons chile powder with lime (such as Tajín®), or more to taste
- 1 lime, or more to taste

Direction

- In a skillet, heat corn on moderate heat for about 5 minutes, until steaming. Take away from the heat and drain water.
- Fill corn halfway into a few mugs or cups. Put each cup with 1-2 tsp chile powder, 1 tbsp. Parmesan cheese and 1 tbsp. mayonnaise, then squeeze lime juice on top.

Nutrition Information

- Calories: 302 calories;
- Total Carbohydrate: 42.4
- Cholesterol: 10

- Protein: 8
- Total Fat: 14.8
- Sodium: 816

20. Fall In Love (with) Guacamole

Serving: 6 | Prep: 15mins | Ready in:

Ingredients

- 3 avocados, peeled and pitted
- 1 teaspoon sea salt
- 1 teaspoon garlic powder
- 2 tablespoons fresh lime juice
- 1/2 cup diced onion
- 2 roma (plum) tomatoes, diced
- 3 tablespoons chopped cilantro
- 1 pinch cayenne pepper, or more to taste (optional)

Direction

- In a bowl, combine together the lime juice, garlic powder, sea salt, and avocados then crush using a fork. Add in the cilantro, tomatoes and onions into the avocado mixture; put cayenne pepper for seasoning.

Nutrition Information

- Calories: 173 calories;
- Sodium: 303
- Total Carbohydrate: 11.5
- Cholesterol: 0
- Protein: 2.5
- Total Fat: 14.8

21. Fiesta Guacamole

Serving: 4 | Prep: 15mins | Ready in:

Ingredients

- 2 ripe avocados, halved and pitted
- 1/4 cup hot salsa
- 1 tablespoon garlic powder
- 1/4 tablespoon chili powder
- 1 1/4 teaspoons hot pepper sauce, or to taste
- 1/2 cup mayonnaise

Direction

- In a bowl, scoop out avocado meat. Use a fork to mash. Mix in hot pepper sauce, chili powder, garlic powder and salsa into the mashed avocados.
- Spread mayonnaise on guacamole. Use plastic wrap to cover bowl. Chill in the fridge for about 1 hour. Mix mayonnaise into guacamole prior to serving.

Nutrition Information

- Calories: 371 calories;
- Total Carbohydrate: 12.3
- Cholesterol: 10
- Protein: 2.9
- Total Fat: 36.7
- Sodium: 304

22. Fresh Tomato Salsa Restaurant Style

Serving: 4 | Prep: 20mins | Ready in:

Ingredients

- 4 large tomatoes, quartered and grated
- 4 scallions (green onions), chopped
- 1 clove garlic, pressed
- 2 slices canned jalapeno pepper, finely chopped
- 1/2 lime, juiced
- 2 tablespoons chopped fresh cilantro, or to taste
- 1/4 teaspoon onion salt
- salt to taste

Direction

- In a bowl, mix jalapeno pepper, garlic, scallions, and tomatoes together. Drizzle with lime juice and add salt, onion salt, and cilantro and mix thoroughly.

Nutrition Information

- Calories: 42 calories;
- Total Carbohydrate: 9.6
- Cholesterol: 0
- Protein: 2
- Total Fat: 0.4
- Sodium: 159

23. Fruit Salsa

Serving: 32 | Prep: 15mins | Ready in:

Ingredients

- 1 tomato
- 1 orange, peeled and segmented
- 2 kiwis, peeled and sliced
- 1 red onion, coarsely chopped
- 1 avocado, peeled and pitted
- 1 bunch cilantro
- 2 jalapeno chile peppers
- garlic salt to taste

Direction

- Put avocado, tomato, jalapeno chile peppers, orange, red onion, kiwis and cilantro in a food processor. Using pulse setting, process until chopped finely but should not be quite smooth. Pour into a medium bowl, and then decorate with the amount of garlic salt desired.

Nutrition Information

- Calories: 18 calories;

- Total Fat: 1
- Sodium: 2
- Total Carbohydrate: 2.4
- Cholesterol: 0
- Protein: 0.3

24. Gravel Salad

Serving: 4 | Prep: 15mins | Ready in:

Ingredients

- 1 cup cooked garbanzo beans
- 1 cup cooked black beans
- 1 cup cooked pinto beans
- 1 cup cooked corn
- 1/2 red bell pepper, chopped
- 1/4 cup chopped fresh chives
- 1/4 cup chopped fresh parsley
- 1/4 cup chopped red onion
- 1 clove garlic, minced
- 3 tablespoons olive oil
- 1 tablespoon red wine vinegar
- salt and pepper to taste

Direction

- Mix together pepper, salt, vinegar, olive oil, garlic, red onion, parsley, chives, red pepper, corn, pinto beans, black beans and garbanzo beans in a big bowl, then blend well together.
- Serve salad with a little toasts spread with sliced tomatoes and olive paste, if you want an elegant and tasty presentation.

Nutrition Information

- Calories: 326 calories;
- Sodium: 408
- Total Carbohydrate: 45.6
- Cholesterol: 0
- Protein: 12.2
- Total Fat: 11.8

25. Healthier Slow Cooker Chicken Tortilla Soup

Serving: 8 | Prep: 40mins | Ready in:

Ingredients

- 1 pound boneless, skinless chicken breasts, cut into strips
- 1 (15 ounce) can whole peeled tomatoes, mashed
- 1 (10 ounce) can enchilada sauce
- 1 medium onion, chopped
- 2 banana peppers, chopped
- 2 cloves garlic, minced
- 2 cups water
- 1 (14.25 ounce) can reduced-sodium chicken broth
- 1 teaspoon cumin
- 1 teaspoon chili powder
- 1 teaspoon salt
- 1/4 teaspoon ground black pepper
- 1 bay leaf
- 1 (10 ounce) package frozen corn
- 1 tablespoon chopped cilantro
- 7 corn tortillas
- vegetable cooking spray

Direction

- In a slow cooker, put the garlic, banana peppers, onion, enchilada sauce, tomatoes and chicken. Pour in chicken broth and water. Put in bay leaf, ground pepper, salt, chili powder and cumin to season, then mix in cilantro and corn. Put cover on and let it cook for 3 to 4 hours on High, or 6-8 hours on Low.
- Set an oven to preheat to 200°C (400°F).
- Use cooking spray to coat both sides of the tortillas lightly. Slice the tortillas into strips, then spread on a baking tray.
- Let them bake in the preheated oven for 10-15 minutes until they become crisp; sprinkle the tortilla strips on top of the soup.

Nutrition Information

- Calories: 208 calories;
- Sodium: 438
- Total Carbohydrate: 23.7
- Cholesterol: 43
- Protein: 15.3
- Total Fat: 6.8

26. Italian Nachos Restaurant Style

Serving: 8 | Prep: 15mins | Ready in:

Ingredients

- 1 pound bulk Italian sausage
- 1 (7-1/2 ounce) bag tortilla chips
- 1 (2 ounce) package sliced pepperoni
- 1/2 pound shredded mozzarella cheese
- 1/2 cup banana peppers, drained
- 1 1/4 cups pizza sauce

Direction

- Preheat the broiler.
- Place a large skillet over medium heat, cook crumbled sausage, stirring, until it is not pink anymore. Drain.
- On a baking sheet, arrange the tortilla chips. Top chips with banana peppers, mozzarella cheese, pepperoni, and the crumbled cooked sausage. Place under the broiler and broil for 5 to 8 minutes, or until the cheese has melted. Serve nachos with a pizza sauce as a dip.

Nutrition Information

- Calories: 453 calories;
- Total Fat: 31.7
- Sodium: 1133
- Total Carbohydrate: 22.5
- Cholesterol: 69
- Protein: 19.3

27. Jalapeno Cream Cheese Chicken Enchiladas

Serving: 7 | Prep: 25mins | Ready in:

Ingredients

- 3 skinless, boneless chicken breast halves
- 1 teaspoon cayenne pepper
- 1/2 teaspoon garlic powder
- salt and ground black pepper to taste
- 2 tablespoons butter
- 1 large onion, minced
- 2 jalapeno peppers, seeded and minced (wear gloves)
- 1 (8 ounce) package cream cheese
- 1 tablespoon garlic powder
- 1/2 teaspoon cayenne pepper
- 1/2 teaspoon paprika
- 1/2 teaspoon chili powder
- 1/2 teaspoon ground cumin
- 1 (28 ounce) can green enchilada sauce
- 7 flour tortillas
- 8 ounces shredded Monterey Jack cheese, divided

Direction

- Set an oven to 175°C (350°F) and start preheating.
- Flavor the chicken breasts with black pepper, salt, 1/2 teaspoon of the garlic powder, and a teaspoon of cayenne pepper. Arrange into a baking dish.
- In the prepared oven, bake for 45 minutes until the chicken is not pink inside and juices from the chicken runs clear. Let the chicken cool and use 2 forks to shred. Put aside the chicken.
- In a large non-stick skillet, heat the butter on medium heat, cook jalapenos and onion for 5 minutes until the onion turns translucent; add in the cream cheese in chunks and stir, let the cream cheese melt and soften. Stir in cumin, chili powder, paprika, cayenne pepper, garlic

powder, and cream cheese. Combine in the cooked chicken meat; then take away from the heat.
- Pour 1/2 of the green enchilada sauce into the bottom of a 9x13-inch baking dish. Place the tortillas on a work surface, then arrange the chicken mixture in a line on the center of each tortilla; then dust each tortilla with 1 tablespoon of Monterey Jack cheese. Roll the tortillas up and arrange seam sides down into the sauce in the dish; pour on the enchiladas with the rest of the sauce. Dust on the top with the rest of 4 ounces of Monterey Jack cheese.
- In the prepared oven, bake for 30-35 minutes until the cheese melts and the filling is bubbly and hot.

Nutrition Information

- Calories: 583 calories;
- Sodium: 599
- Total Carbohydrate: 38.4
- Cholesterol: 123
- Protein: 28.7
- Total Fat: 35.5

28. Jicama Mango Slaw

Serving: 6 | Prep: 25mins | Ready in:

Ingredients

- 2 mangos, peeled and cut into matchstick julienne
- 1 carrot, cut into matchstick julienne
- 1 red bell pepper, cut into matchstick julienne
- 1/2 large jicama, peeled and cut into matchstick julienne
- 1 tablespoon raspberry vinegar
- 1 tablespoon lime juice
- 1 tablespoon agave nectar
- 1 tablespoon olive oil
- 1 tablespoon minced fresh mint
- 1 teaspoon lime zest

Direction

- In a big bowl, mix the carrot, jicama, red bell pepper and mangos together. In another bowl, stir in the olive oil, lime juice, vinegar and agave nectar. Pour dressing over the mango mixture. Sprinkle with lime zest and mint then toss to coat evenly. Store in the refrigerator for at least 30 minutes before serving.

Nutrition Information

- Calories: 114 calories;
- Total Fat: 2.6
- Sodium: 15
- Total Carbohydrate: 23
- Cholesterol: 0
- Protein: 1.3

29. Jicama Salad With Cilantro And Lime

Serving: 8 | Prep: 10mins | Ready in:

Ingredients

- 2 pounds jicama, peeled and julienned
- 1/4 cup chopped cilantro leaves
- salt and pepper to taste
- 1/4 cup lime juice

Direction

- Combine pepper, salt, chopped cilantro, and julienned jicama in a big bowl. Sprinkle lime juice then toss to coat. Keep in fridge until ready to serve.

Nutrition Information

- Calories: 46 calories;
- Protein: 0.9
- Total Fat: 0.1
- Sodium: 5

- Total Carbohydrate: 10.9
- Cholesterol: 0

30. Jim's Pork Chorizo

Serving: 6 | Prep: 15mins | Ready in:

Ingredients

- 2 pounds ground pork
- 2 teaspoons salt
- 4 tablespoons chili powder
- 1/4 teaspoon ground cloves
- 2 tablespoons paprika
- 2 cloves garlic, crushed
- 1 teaspoon dried oregano
- 3 1/2 tablespoons cider vinegar

Direction

- Combine vinegar, oregano, garlic, paprika, ground cloves, chili powder, salt, and ground pork well. Put in an air-tight container to store in the fridge for the spices to combine before using, about 4 days.

Nutrition Information

- Calories: 338 calories;
- Sodium: 906
- Total Carbohydrate: 4.8
- Cholesterol: 98
- Protein: 27.9
- Total Fat: 22.9

31. Jimmy Dean 6 Layer Breakfast Casserole

Serving: 4 | Prep: | Ready in:

Ingredients

- 6 whole eggs
- 1/4 cup heavy cream
- 1 teaspoon salt
- 1/4 teaspoon black pepper, ground
- 1 (16 ounce) package Jimmy Dean Hot Roll Sausage, cooked, crumbled, drained
- 1/4 cup jalapeno pepper, 1/4 inch dice
- 1/2 cup Cheddar cheese, shredded
- 2 tablespoons garlic, minced
- 1 teaspoon cumin, ground
- 4 slices bread, 1/2 inch thick slices

Direction

- Start preheating the oven to 350°F. In a bowl, start by stirring heavy cream and eggs with pepper and salt.
- Put cumin, garlic, cheese, jalapeno pepper, and sausage in another bowl.
- On the bottom of a 2-qt. baking dish, put 1/3 the egg mixture. And then, add a bread slice to the dish. Put 1/3 the sausage mixture from step 2 onto the bread slice.
- Redo step 3 to 4 until the last bread slice is on top. Evenly put across the top bread slice with the leftover 1/3 sausage ingredients. Put in the oven and bake for 15 minutes.

Nutrition Information

32. Jimmy's Mexican Pizza

Serving: 8 | Prep: 20mins | Ready in:

Ingredients

- 1/2 pound ground beef
- 1 medium onion, diced
- 1 clove garlic, minced
- 1 tablespoon chili powder
- 1 teaspoon ground cumin
- 1/2 teaspoon paprika
- 1/2 teaspoon black pepper

- 1/2 teaspoon salt
- 1 (16 ounce) can refried beans
- 4 (10 inch) flour tortillas
- 1/2 cup salsa
- 1 cup shredded Cheddar cheese
- 1 cup shredded Monterey Jack cheese
- 2 green onions, chopped
- 2 roma (plum) tomatoes, diced
- 1/4 cup thinly sliced jalapeno pepper
- 1/4 cup sour cream (optional)

Direction

- Start preheating oven to 350°F (175°C). Coat non-stick cooking spray over two pie plates.
- In a skillet, put garlic, onion and beef over medium heat. Then cook until the beef is browned evenly. Drain the grease off. Add pepper, salt, paprika, cumin and chili powder to season the meat.
- In each pie plate, lay 1 tortilla. Cover with 1 refried beans layer. Spread over each one with 1/2 seasoned ground beef. Cover with the second tortilla. Bake in prepared oven for 10 mins.
- Take plates out of the oven. Allow to cool slightly. Spread onto each top of tortilla with 1/2 salsa. Add 1/2 Cheddar and Monterey Jack cheeses to cover each pizza. Top each one with 1/2 tomatoes, 1/2 green onions and 1/2 jalapeno slices.
- Put pizzas back to oven. Bake until cheese melts, about 5-10 mins more. Take out of the oven. Allow to cool slightly. Then slice each one into four pieces.

Nutrition Information

- Calories: 370 calories;
- Cholesterol: 55
- Protein: 19.6
- Total Fat: 18.6
- Sodium: 848
- Total Carbohydrate: 31.6

33. Ken's Kickin' Posole

Serving: 12 | Prep: 20mins | Ready in:

Ingredients

- 2 fresh poblano chile peppers
- 8 ounces bacon, chopped
- 1 tablespoon bacon drippings
- 2 pounds pork loin, cut into 1-inch cubes
- 1 onion, diced
- 10 cloves garlic, minced
- 2 jalapeno peppers, seeded and diced
- 1 teaspoon dried Mexican oregano
- 2 teaspoons ground cumin
- 1 teaspoon New Mexico chile powder
- 1/4 teaspoon ground cloves
- 1/2 teaspoon kosher salt
- 1 bunch cilantro, chopped
- 8 cups chicken stock
- 1 (14.5 ounce) can mild red enchilada sauce
- 2 (29 ounce) cans white hominy, rinsed and drained

Direction

- Start preheating the oven's broiler and put the oven rack approximately 6 inches from the heat source. Use aluminum foil to line a baking sheet. Put poblano chiles with the cut side turning down onto the baking sheet.
- Put under the preheated broiler and cook for 5 minutes until the skin of the peppers become blistered and blackened. In a bowl, put the blackened peppers, and cover tightly with plastic wrap. Let the peppers steam for 20 minutes while they cool. When cool, peel the skins and dispose. Dice the chiles.
- In a big pot, stir and cook bacon over medium heat for 5 minutes until the bacon starts to become crunchy and release its fat. Put the bacon on a dish lined with paper towel to strain, dispose all but save 1 tablespoon of bacon grease from the pot. Raise the heat to medium-high, and add the pork loin cubes. Cook for 5 minutes, mixing sometimes until all sides turn brown. Take the pork out of the pot

and lower the heat to medium. Mix in garlic and onion, stir and cook for 5 minutes until the onion is starting to turn brown and tender.
- Mix cilantro, salt, cloves, New Mexico chile powder, cumin, oregano, jalapeno peppers, and the roasted poblano chiles into the onions, cook for 1 minute. Add the enchilada sauce and chicken stock. Mix in pork cubes and bacon, and simmer over medium-high heat. Lower the heat to medium-low, put a cover on and simmer for 1 hour. Mix in hominy, cover again and keep cooking for another 1 hour until the pork is very soft.

Nutrition Information

- Calories: 336 calories;
- Total Carbohydrate: 26.7
- Cholesterol: 56
- Protein: 21
- Total Fat: 15.8
- Sodium: 1103

34. Margarita Con Cerveza

Serving: 8 | Prep: 10mins | Ready in:

Ingredients

- 1 (12 fluid ounce) can frozen limeade concentrate
- 1 (12 fluid ounce) can or bottle Mexican beer (such as Corona®)
- 1 (12 fluid ounce) can or bottle lemon-lime soda (such as 7-Up®)
- 1 cup tequila
- 1/2 cup triple sec
- 1 lime, halved

Direction

- Into a pitcher, add limeade concentrate and then mix to break into big chunks. Add triple sec, beer, tequila, and lemon-lime soda. Mix thoroughly. Press 1/2 lime into the margarita. Chop the remaining lime half into wedges and use them to decorate margarita glasses.

Nutrition Information

- Calories: 297 calories;
- Total Fat: 0.1
- Sodium: 8
- Total Carbohydrate: 48.3
- Cholesterol: 0
- Protein: 0.3

35. Marinated Flank Steak

Serving: 6 | Prep: 15mins | Ready in:

Ingredients

- 1/2 cup vegetable oil
- 1/3 cup soy sauce
- 1/4 cup red wine vinegar
- 2 tablespoons fresh lemon juice
- 1 1/2 tablespoons Worcestershire sauce
- 1 tablespoon Dijon mustard
- 2 cloves garlic, minced
- 1/2 teaspoon ground black pepper
- 1 1/2 pounds flank steak

Direction

- Combine the lemon juice, mustard, soy sauce, Worcestershire sauce, vinegar, oil, ground black pepper and garlic together in a medium-sized bowl. In a shallow glass dish, put in the steak. Put the marinade mixture on top of the steak and turn the steak until well-coated with marinade. Cover the marinated steak and keep it in the fridge for 6 hours.
- Preheat the grill to medium-high heat.
- Grease the grill grate with oil. Put the steaks onto the preheated grill and throw away the marinade mixture. Let it cook on the grill for 5 minutes on every side until the preferred doneness is achieved.

Nutrition Information

- Calories: 275 calories;
- Sodium: 935
- Total Carbohydrate: 3.4
- Cholesterol: 27
- Protein: 14.8
- Total Fat: 22.5

36. Menudo

Serving: 7 | Prep: | Ready in:

Ingredients

- 2 pounds beef tripe
- 2 onions, chopped
- 4 (15 ounce) cans white hominy
- 1/4 teaspoon chili powder
- salt and pepper to taste

Direction

- Mix the onions and tripe together in a 16-quart pot. Pour in water to cover 3/4 of the pot. Let cook while covered over low heat until the tripe gets tender, about 2 hours. Add the pepper, salt, chili powder and hominy for seasoning. Let cook while covered for 45 to 60 more minutes for the flavors to combine together. Use lemon, corn tortillas and fresh onions to serve if preferred.

Nutrition Information

- Calories: 296 calories;
- Sodium: 632
- Total Carbohydrate: 37.2
- Cholesterol: 158
- Protein: 19.6
- Total Fat: 6.9

37. Mexi Hominy

Serving: 4 | Prep: 15mins | Ready in:

Ingredients

- 2 (15.5 ounce) cans white or yellow hominy, rinsed and drained
- 1 (16 ounce) can diced tomatoes
- 1 (4.5 ounce) can diced green chiles
- 1 teaspoon ground cumin
- 1 clove minced garlic
- chopped fresh cilantro
- salt and pepper to taste
- shredded Monterey Jack cheese (optional)

Direction

- Combine garlic, cumin, green chiles, tomatoes and hominy in a saucepan; put over medium heat. Let it cook for about 7 minutes. Add cilantro and stir. Take it off the heat and distribute to bowls. Use cheese to top.

Nutrition Information

- Calories: 246 calories;
- Sodium: 1096
- Total Carbohydrate: 37.6
- Cholesterol: 13
- Protein: 8.2
- Total Fat: 6.4

38. Mexican Chicken Crepes

Serving: 8 | Prep: 35mins | Ready in:

Ingredients

- 1 cup milk
- 3 eggs
- 2 tablespoons vegetable oil, divided
- 3 tablespoons all-purpose flour

- 1/4 teaspoon salt
- 2 1/2 cups shredded pepper Jack cheese, divided
- 1 1/2 cups diced cooked chicken
- 1 cup low-fat sour cream
- 2 green onions, sliced
- 1 small jalapeno pepper, chopped
- 4 cloves garlic, chopped
- 1 teaspoon chili powder
- 1 teaspoon ground cumin

Direction

- Start preheating oven to 350°F (175°C).
- In a bowl, mix 1 1/2 tablespoons oil, eggs, and milk together. Add salt and flour.
- In a skillet, heat the remaining oil over medium heat. Add about 1/4 cup batter. Cook for 3 mins until brown. Turn and cook for 2 mins longer, until the other side is brown. Take out crepe and cool. Repeat with remaining batter.
- In a bowl, stir cumin, chili powder, garlic, jalapeno, green onions, sour cream, chicken and pepper Jack cheese together. Spoon half cup of the mixture onto the middle of each crepe. Roll and put, seam-side down, in a single layer in a shallow baking pan (about 9x13-inch). Top with a sprinkle of remaining pepper Jack cheese.
- Bake for 20-30 mins in the prepared oven or until bubbly and golden brown.

Nutrition Information

- Calories: 340 calories;
- Total Fat: 24.9
- Sodium: 395
- Total Carbohydrate: 7.7
- Cholesterol: 148
- Protein: 20.9

39. Mexican Corn Bread Casserole

Serving: 8 | Prep: 15mins | Ready in:

Ingredients

- Meat Base:
- 1 tablespoon olive oil
- 1 small onion, diced
- 1/2 red bell pepper, chopped
- 1 pound ground beef
- 1 teaspoon minced garlic
- 1 teaspoon chili powder
- 1/4 teaspoon cayenne pepper
- salt and ground black pepper to taste
- 1/2 cup frozen corn
- 1 cup shredded Mexican cheese blend, divided, or more to taste
- 1 cup salsa
- Corn Bread Topping:
- 1 cup cornmeal
- 3/4 teaspoon salt
- 1/2 teaspoon baking soda
- 1 cup milk
- 2 eggs, beaten

Direction

- Set the oven to 425°F (220°C) and start preheating.
- In a skillet, heat olive oil over medium-high heat. Add red bell pepper and onion; sauté for 5-7 minutes until softened. Add black pepper, salt, cayenne pepper, chili powder, garlic and ground beef. Cook while stirring for 5-7 minutes until beef turned browned and crumbly.
- Combine corn into the beef mixture; toss for about 3 minutes to defrost. Drain; get rid of fat. Add about 1/4 of the shredded Mexican cheese blend; combine well. Place meat sauce into a 9x13-inch casserole dish. Place a thin salsa layer on top of meat to cover.
- In a large bowl, mix baking soda, salt and cornmeal. Add eggs and milk; stir until blended well. Place cornmeal mixture over

layer of salsa; arrange the rest of shredded Mexican cheese blend on top.
- Bake in the prepared oven for about half an hour until top turns browned.

Nutrition Information

- Calories: 304 calories;
- Total Fat: 16.3
- Sodium: 708
- Total Carbohydrate: 21.5
- Cholesterol: 101
- Protein: 18.2

40. Mexican Mole Sauce

Serving: 4 | Prep: 10mins | Ready in:

Ingredients

- 2 teaspoons vegetable oil
- 1/4 cup finely chopped onion
- 1 tablespoon unsweetened cocoa powder
- 1 teaspoon ground cumin
- 1 teaspoon dried cilantro
- 1/8 tablespoon dried minced garlic
- 1 (10.75 ounce) can condensed tomato soup
- 1 (4 ounce) can diced green chile peppers

Direction

- In a medium saucepan, heat oil on moderate heat and cook onion until softened. Blend in garlic, cilantro, cumin and cocoa powder, then stir in green chile peppers and tomato soup. Bring the mixture to a boil, then lower heat to low and simmer, covered, for 10 minutes. Pour over food directly to serve or transfer the sauce to a gravy boat.

Nutrition Information

- Calories: 88 calories;
- Total Carbohydrate: 13.7
- Cholesterol: 0
- Protein: 2
- Total Fat: 3.8
- Sodium: 753

41. Mexican Pot Roast

Serving: 12 | Prep: 15mins | Ready in:

Ingredients

- 2 tablespoons olive oil
- 1 (4 pound) beef chuck roast, trimmed
- 1 teaspoon salt
- 1 teaspoon ground black pepper
- 1 large onion, chopped
- 1 1/4 cups diced green chile pepper
- 1 (5 ounce) bottle hot sauce
- 1/4 cup taco seasoning
- 1 teaspoon chili powder
- 1 teaspoon cayenne pepper
- 1 teaspoon garlic powder

Direction

- In a big skillet, heat the olive oil over medium-high heat. Use salt and pepper to season the beef chuck roast then cook it in hot oil for 2 to 3 minutes on each side. When it has browned entirely, move it to a slow cooker.
- Sprinkle garlic powder, cayenne pepper, chilli powder, taco seasoning, hot sauce, chile pepper and onion over the roast and cook it on low. Let it cook for 8 to 10 hours until the meat is fall-apart tender.

Nutrition Information

- Calories: 213 calories;
- Cholesterol: 70
- Protein: 21.2
- Total Fat: 11.2
- Sodium: 772
- Total Carbohydrate: 5.4

42. Mexican Taco Quinoa Bowl With Chicken

Serving: 6 | Prep: 10mins | Ready in:

Ingredients

- 1 cup quinoa
- 2 cups water
- 1 (15 ounce) can black beans, drained
- 1 (15 ounce) can tomato sauce
- 1 onion, chopped
- 1 tablespoon chili powder
- 1 1/2 teaspoons ground cumin
- 1 teaspoon sea salt
- 1 teaspoon ground black pepper
- 1/2 teaspoon paprika
- 1/4 teaspoon garlic powder
- 1/4 teaspoon onion powder
- 1/4 teaspoon red pepper flakes
- 1/4 teaspoon dried oregano
- 1 tablespoon olive oil
- 1 1/2 pounds chicken breasts, cubed

Direction

- Place a saucepan over medium heat; put in dry quinoa. Stir for 3-5 minutes, or till fragrant and toasted. Put in oregano, red pepper flakes, onion powder, garlic powder, paprika, pepper, salt, cumin, chili powder, onion, tomato sauce, black beans and water. Boil the mixture. Turn the heat down to low; simmer for 20-25 minutes, till the quinoa turns tender.
- Place a skillet on medium heat; heat olive oil. Put in chicken; cook while stirring for 6-8 minutes, till not pink in the center anymore and browned on the outside.
- Using a fork, fluff the cooked quinoa mixture. Distribute into serving bowls. Place the cooked chicken on top.

Nutrition Information

- Calories: 355 calories;
- Cholesterol: 65
- Protein: 33.6
- Total Fat: 7.5
- Sodium: 1008
- Total Carbohydrate: 38.8

43. Mexican Vegetable Rice Bowl

Serving: 2 | Prep: 15mins | Ready in:

Ingredients

- 4 teaspoons liquid amino acid (such as Bragg®), divided
- 1/4 teaspoon onion powder
- 1 large zucchini, diced small
- 2 large kale leaves, cut into 1-inch squares
- 1/2 (14 ounce) can coconut milk
- 1/2 cup raw macadamia nuts
- 1/4 cup raw cashews
- 1/4 cup nutritional yeast
- 2 teaspoons chili powder
- 1 pinch cayenne pepper, or to taste
- 1 pinch red pepper flakes, or to taste
- 1 teaspoon vegetable oil
- 1 cup hot cooked brown rice

Direction

- In a small bowl, stir together onion powder and 1 tablespoon of liquid amino acid, dissolving the powder, then pour into a big resealable plastic bag. Add kale and zucchini, working the bag to coat with marinade. Squeeze out the excess air from the bag and seal. Marinate the vegetables for about 10-15 minutes.
- In a blender, blend together red pepper flakes, cayenne pepper, the leftover liquid amino acid, chili powder, nutritional yeast, cashews, macadamia nuts, and coconut milk until the mixture is smooth.
- Heat the oil in a big pan over medium-high heat, and pour in the kale and zucchini from

the plastic bag, then sauté for 2-3 minutes until they are heated through.
- Divide the cooked rice into 2 bowls and top each with half the vegetable mixture, then drizzle with the blended sauce.

Nutrition Information

- Calories: 772 calories;
- Total Fat: 59.1
- Sodium: 469
- Total Carbohydrate: 53.3
- Cholesterol: 0
- Protein: 22.1

44. Mexican Zucchini Cheese Soup

Serving: 6 | Prep: 20mins | Ready in:

Ingredients

- 1 tablespoon olive oil
- 1 cup chopped onion
- 2 cloves garlic, minced
- 1/2 teaspoon dried oregano
- 2 (14.5 ounce) cans chicken broth
- 1 (14.5 ounce) can Mexican-style stewed tomatoes
- 2 medium zucchini, halved lengthwise and cut in 1/4 inch slices
- 2 medium yellow squash, halved lengthwise and cut in 1/4 inch slices
- 1 (8.75 ounce) can whole kernel corn, drained
- 1 (4.5 ounce) can diced green chile peppers
- 12 ounces processed cheese food, cubed
- 1/2 teaspoon freshly ground black pepper
- 1/4 cup chopped fresh cilantro

Direction

- In a big pot, heat olive oil, and sauté garlic and onion until soft. Use oregano to season.
- Stir in tomatoes and chicken broth. Boil it. Stir in chile peppers, corn, yellow squash, and zucchini. Lower the heat to low, and simmer until the squash is soft, about 10 minutes.
- Stir cubed processed cheese into the soup. Keep stirring and cooking until the cheese melts. Use pepper to season. Stir in cilantro right before eating.

Nutrition Information

- Calories: 307 calories;
- Cholesterol: 48
- Protein: 14.7
- Total Fat: 17.5
- Sodium: 1829
- Total Carbohydrate: 26.2

45. Mommy's Lemonade (Margaritas)

Serving: 12 | Prep: 5mins | Ready in:

Ingredients

- 1 (12 fluid ounce) can frozen limeade concentrate (such as Minute Maid®), thawed
- 3 (12 fluid ounce) cans cold water
- 1 (12 fluid ounce) can tequila (such as Cuervo® Especial)
- 1/2 (12 fluid ounce) can brandy-based orange liqueur (such as Grand Marnier®)
- ice cubes
- kosher salt for rimming glasses (optional)
- 1 lime, cut into wedges (optional)

Direction

- In a pitcher, pour in limeade concentrate. Fill the can with cold water and pour it into the pitcher. Do the same steps twice to have a total of 3 cans of water. Pour tequila into the can and pour it into the pitcher. Pour orange liqueur into the can, filling it halfway, and pour the liqueur into the pitcher. Mix well. Let it chill thoroughly. Serve the drink in a salt-rimmed glass filled with ice and with a lime wedge.

Nutrition Information

- Calories: 207 calories;
- Protein: 0
- Total Fat: 0.1
- Sodium: 38
- Total Carbohydrate: 29.5
- Cholesterol: 0

46. My Ultimate Guacamole

Serving: 6 | Prep: 20mins | Ready in:

Ingredients

- 3 avocados, peeled and pitted
- 1 (16 ounce) package cottage cheese
- 1 large tomato, chopped
- 1 (4 ounce) can chopped green chilies
- 1 lime, juiced
- 1/2 teaspoon garlic powder
- 1/2 teaspoon salt
- 1/4 teaspoon ground black pepper

Direction

- Get a bowl and put in avocados then crush until texture becomes creamy; but leave a few chunks. Add in the black pepper, salt, garlic powder, lime juice, green chilies, tomato and cottage cheese until well combined. Let it chill inside the refrigerator for about 10 minutes.

Nutrition Information

- Calories: 250 calories;
- Total Fat: 18.2
- Sodium: 724
- Total Carbohydrate: 13.5
- Cholesterol: 11
- Protein: 11.8

47. Nacho Tacos

Serving: 8 | Prep: 10mins | Ready in:

Ingredients

- 1 pound ground beef
- 1 medium onion, chopped
- 1/2 teaspoon chili powder
- 1 (10.75 ounce) can Campbell's® Condensed Fiesta Nacho Cheese Soup
- 8 taco shells, warmed
- 1 cup shredded lettuce
- 1 medium tomato, chopped

Direction

- In one 10 inches skillet on moderately-high heat, cook the chili powder, onion and beef till beef is nicely browned, mixing frequently to crumble meat. Drain any fat.
- In skillet, mix half a cup of soup and cook till mixture is bubbling and hot.
- In a one-quart saucepan on moderately-high heat, heat the rest of the soup until bubbling and hot. Into taco shells, scoop beef mixture. Put tomato, lettuce and soup on top.

Nutrition Information

- Calories: 219 calories;
- Total Carbohydrate: 14.7
- Cholesterol: 39
- Protein: 11.9
- Total Fat: 12.5
- Sodium: 337

48. Peanut Butter Banana Quesadilla

Serving: 2 | Prep: 10mins | Ready in:

Ingredients

- 1/4 cup peanut butter
- 2 (8 inch) flour tortillas
- 1 banana, sliced
- cooking spray

Direction

- Smear 1/2 of the peanut butter over one side of a flour tortilla, and place sliced banana over. Smear the rest of peanut butter over one side of another flour tortilla; place the second tortilla on top of banana slices, peanut butter-side down.
- Grease a skillet with cooking spray and set over medium heat. Arrange quesadilla into the heated skillet and cook, about 3 minutes on each side, until lightly brown. Cut quesadillas into 2 pieces to serve.

Nutrition Information

- Calories: 403 calories;
- Total Carbohydrate: 47
- Cholesterol: 0
- Protein: 13
- Total Fat: 20.1
- Sodium: 383

49. Pie Iron Tacos

Serving: 6 | Prep: 15mins | Ready in:

Ingredients

- 1 pound ground beef
- 1 (1 ounce) package taco seasoning mix
- 12 (5 inch) corn tortillas
- 1 cup shredded Monterey Jack cheese
- 1/2 cup chopped onion
- 2 cups shredded iceberg lettuce
- 1 large tomato, diced
- 1 (8 ounce) jar salsa
- 1 (8 ounce) container sour cream (optional)

Direction

- Cook ground beef in big skillet on medium high heat till browned, mixing to crumble. Pour excess fat off; follow package directions to mix taco seasoning in.
- Spray cooking spray inside pie iron; on 1 side, put corn tortilla. Put scoop of ground beef over tortilla then sprinkle chopped onion and Monterey jack cheese. Put 2nd tortilla over; close pie iron.
- Cook taco above moderate campfire coals till taco is hot in middle and tortillas are browned and crisped. Serve with sour cream, salsa, tomato and lettuce; repeat with leftover ingredients.

Nutrition Information

- Calories: 430 calories;
- Total Carbohydrate: 31.8
- Cholesterol: 79
- Protein: 22.4
- Total Fat: 24
- Sodium: 759

50. Pollo Con Nopales (Chicken And Cactus)

Serving: 2 | Prep: 10mins | Ready in:

Ingredients

- 2 skinless, boneless chicken breast halves
- 3 fresh tomatillos, husks removed
- 3 fresh jalapeno peppers, seeded
- 1 (16 ounce) jar canned nopales (cactus), drained

Direction

- Bring a pot of water to a boil. Add chicken breasts to the boiling water; cook for 10 minutes, or until juices run clear and the center is no longer pink. Pierce the center with an instant-read thermometer, it should read at least 74°C/165°F. Drain and set aside to allow chicken to cool. Once cool enough to handle, shred into small strands.

- Fill the pot with water again and bring to a boil. Add nopales, jalapeno peppers, and tomatillos in the boiling water; cook for 5 minutes, or until vegetables are tender. Drain.
- In a blender, add the jalapeno peppers and tomatillos. Blend until mixture is smooth, then pour into the pot with shredded chicken. Place the pot over medium heat. Dice the nopales into small pieces and add to the mixture. Simmer for 5 minutes, or until the mixture is completely reheated.

Nutrition Information

- Calories: 174 calories;
- Cholesterol: 59
- Protein: 25.7
- Total Fat: 3.2
- Sodium: 99
- Total Carbohydrate: 11.9

51. Prickly Pear Cactus Margarita

Serving: 1 | Prep: 10mins | Ready in:

Ingredients

- coarse salt as needed
- 2 fluid ounces tequila
- 2 fluid ounces sweet and sour mix
- 1 fluid ounce triple sec
- 1 fluid ounce lime juice
- 1 fluid ounce prickly pear syrup

Direction

- Put salt in a small plate. Moisten the lip of a margarita glass; press in the plate of salt.
- Put ice in a cocktail shaker until full. Add in pear syrup, tequila, lime juice, sweet and sour mix, and triple sec; cover and shake the cocktail shaker well. Filter cocktail in the prepared margarita glass.

Nutrition Information

- Calories: 423 calories;
- Sodium: 3
- Total Carbohydrate: 56.3
- Cholesterol: 0
- Protein: 0.1
- Total Fat: 0.1

52. Quesadillas De Los Bajos

Serving: 4 | Prep: 30mins | Ready in:

Ingredients

- 3 green chile peppers
- Pico de Gallo:
- 1 green bell pepper, halved, divided
- 2 small tomatoes, diced
- 1 small onion, divided
- 3 fresh jalapeno peppers, diced
- 2 tablespoons chopped fresh cilantro
- 2 tablespoons tomato juice
- 1 lime, juiced
- 1 clove garlic, minced
- 1/2 teaspoon salt
- 1/2 teaspoon ground black pepper
- 1/4 teaspoon garlic salt
- Filling:
- 3 tablespoons extra-light olive oil, divided
- 2 cooked skinless, boneless chicken breast halves, diced
- 7 mushrooms, sliced
- 1 tablespoon chili powder
- 1/2 teaspoon dried oregano
- 1 pinch garlic salt
- 1 pinch ground black pepper
- 1/3 cup red enchilada sauce, or more to taste
- Quesadilla:
- 1/2 cup shredded pepperjack cheese

- 1/2 cup shredded Cheddar cheese
- 4 (10 inch) flour tortillas

Direction

- Position the oven rack 6 inches away from heat source. Turn on the oven's broiler to preheat. On baking sheet, place green chile peppers.
- Put peppers into preheated oven to roast for 5-10 minutes, flipping 1 or 2 times, until skins are blackened and charred. Pour into a resealable bag and seal; set aside for 10 minutes until the steam begins to peel the skins off. Unseal the bag carefully; remove pepper skins. Dice peppers.
- Dice 2/3 of the onion and 1/2 of the bell pepper; in a bowl, combine with 1/4 teaspoon of garlic salt, 1/2 teaspoon of black pepper, salt, garlic, lime juice, tomato juice, cilantro, jalapeno pepper and tomatoes. Put pico de gallo into the refrigerator with a cover.
- In a skillet, heat 1 tablespoon of olive oil over medium heat. Slice the remaining 1/2 of bell pepper and 1/3 of the onion thinly; combine with mushrooms and chicken and cook in hot oil while stirring for 5-10 minutes until the vegetables are just softened. Put in 1 pinch of black pepper, 1 pinch of garlic salt, oregano, chili powder and roasted green chile peppers; cook for 30 seconds while stirring until fragrant. Coat the vegetable mixture by stirring in enough enchilada sauce.
- Use Cheddar cheese and pepperjack cheese to spread onto 1/2 of each tortilla. Add a layer of vegetable mixture over cheese layer and spread out. Fold each tortilla over the layer of vegetable and cheese. Use the remaining 2 tablespoons of olive oil to brush outsides of tortillas.
- In a skillet or a sandwich press, cook quesadillas in batches on medium heat for 2 minutes, until browned and the cheeses melt. Slice into 4 wedges. Serve together with pico de gallo.

Nutrition Information

- Calories: 706 calories;
- Sodium: 1301
- Total Carbohydrate: 52
- Cholesterol: 115
- Protein: 46.6
- Total Fat: 35.4

53. Quick And Easy Taco Dip

Serving: 20 | Prep: 10mins | Ready in:

Ingredients

- 1 (8 ounce) package cream cheese, softened
- 3/4 teaspoon taco seasoning mix
- 1/3 cup salsa
- 1 (8 ounce) package shredded Cheddar cheese

Direction

- Combine salsa, taco seasoning mix and cream cheese in a medium bowl. Spread the mixture into an 8-in. baking pan or a shallow serving dish. Place Cheddar cheese on top, then refrigerate in the fridge for an hour before serving.

Nutrition Information

- Calories: 86 calories;
- Total Carbohydrate: 0.8
- Cholesterol: 24
- Protein: 3.7
- Total Fat: 7.6
- Sodium: 137

54. Red Pepper Chicken

Serving: 2 | Prep: 15mins | Ready in:

Ingredients

- 1 cup water
- 1/2 cup uncooked long grain white rice
- 1 tablespoon extra virgin olive oil
- 4 fluid ounces Mexican beer
- 2 boneless, skinless chicken breast halves
- 2 tablespoons chili powder
- 1 tablespoon dried oregano
- salt and pepper to taste
- 1/2 red bell pepper, chopped
- 1 fresh red chile pepper, finely chopped
- 1/2 clove garlic, minced
- 1/2 lime, thinly sliced
- 1/2 lemon, thinly sliced
- 1/4 cup grated Romano cheese

Direction

- Boil water and rice in a saucepan. Put cover, lower heat, and let simmer till rice is soft for 25 minutes.
- In a skillet over medium heat, heat the 1 fluid ounce beer and olive oil. In the skillet put the chicken, and add pepper, salt, oregano and chili powder to season. Mix in the lemon, lime, garlic, chile pepper, red bell pepper and leftover beer. Cook till juices run clear and chicken is no longer pink for 15 minutes.
- Put the vegetables and chicken on top of the cooked rice, put Romano cheese over and serve.

Nutrition Information

- Calories: 505 calories;
- Sodium: 317
- Total Carbohydrate: 56.2
- Cholesterol: 76
- Protein: 34.1
- Total Fat: 15.4

55. Red Ribbon Roasted Salsa

Serving: 12 | Prep: 20mins | Ready in:

Ingredients

- 10 dried chipotle peppers
- 12 roma (plum) tomatoes
- 1/4 yellow onion, coarsely chopped
- 2 cloves garlic, or more to taste
- 2 tablespoons white vinegar
- 2 teaspoons salt
- 1 pinch ground black pepper, or to taste (optional)
- 1 lime, juiced, or more to taste (optional)

Direction

- Fill water into a saucepan. Mix in dried chipotle peppers and bring to a boil. Lower heat to low and simmer for 30 minutes until peppers are soft. Then Drain and let cool. Remove stems, cut peppers open, and remove seeds when peppers are cool. Put aside peppers.
- Preheat outdoor grill to high heat. Lightly oil the grate.
- On hot grate, grill tomatoes for 10 minutes until skin begins to peel and blackens, turning tomatoes often so all sides blacken. Put grilled tomatoes aside. Cool.
- In a food processor, pulse lime juice, black pepper, salt, white vinegar, yellow onion, chipotle peppers and grilled tomatoes several times. Process until nearly pureed.
- Refrigerate for 2 hours to overnight until flavors merge.

Nutrition Information

- Calories: 16 calories;
- Total Fat: 0.2
- Sodium: 391
- Total Carbohydrate: 3.7
- Cholesterol: 0
- Protein: 0.7

56. Restaurant Style Cheesy Poblano Pepper Soup

Serving: 9 | Prep: 20mins | Ready in:

Ingredients

- 3 (6 inch) corn tortillas
- 2 tablespoons all-purpose flour
- 1/2 teaspoon chili powder
- 1 teaspoon ground cumin
- 1/2 teaspoon salt
- 1/2 teaspoon ground black pepper
- 2 tablespoons vegetable oil
- 1/2 cup chopped onion
- 1/2 cup fresh poblano chile pepper, seeded and minced
- 1/2 teaspoon minced garlic
- 2 tablespoons margarine
- 2 cups chicken stock
- 1/2 cup half-and-half
- 1/8 cup cooked and chopped chicken
- 1/2 cup shredded Monterey Jack cheese
- 1/2 cup fresh poblano chile pepper, seeded and chopped
- 6 (6 inch) corn tortillas, cut into strips and toasted for garnish

Direction

- Break the corn tortillas into ninths then put them into a food processor and crush until fine. Add the chili powder, cumin, flour, salt and pepper. Continue to process until you achieve a texture similar to cornmeal. Lay to one side.
- Set a big pot over medium heat and combine oil, garlic, onion and 1/2 cup poblano chile peppers. Sauté until onions are transparent, about 5 minutes. Mix in margarine or butter and continue to cook until it melts. Pour the ground tortilla mixture into the pot and blend well using a wire whisk to form a roux. Make sure not to let the mixture burn.
- Stirring continuously, slowly pour in chicken stock. Make sure to scour the sides and bottom of the pot as you stir. Pour in the half-and-half and slowly cook to a simmer for about 7 to 10 minutes. Don't let soup come to a boil.
- Switch off the heat and set soup aside to cool a bit. When serving, add chicken to the soup and arrange poblano chili peppers, tortilla strips and cheese on top of each serving for garnish.

Nutrition Information

- Calories: 168 calories;
- Sodium: 366
- Total Carbohydrate: 15.7
- Cholesterol: 12
- Protein: 4.8
- Total Fat: 10.1

57. Restaurant Style Tequila Lime Chicken

Serving: 4 | Prep: 30mins | Ready in:

Ingredients

- Chicken Marinade:
- 1 cup water
- 1/3 cup teriyaki sauce
- 2 tablespoons lime juice
- 2 teaspoons minced garlic
- 1 teaspoon liquid smoke flavoring
- 1/2 teaspoon salt
- 1/4 teaspoon ground ginger
- 1/4 teaspoon tequila
- 4 skinless, boneless chicken breast halves
- Mexi-Ranch Dressing:
- 1/4 cup mayonnaise
- 1/4 cup sour cream
- 1 tablespoon milk
- 2 teaspoons minced tomato
- 1 1/2 teaspoons chopped green chile peppers
- 1 teaspoon minced onion
- 1/4 teaspoon dried parsley
- 1/4 teaspoon hot pepper sauce

- 1 pinch salt
- 1 pinch dried dill weed
- 1 pinch paprika
- 1 pinch cayenne pepper
- 1 pinch ground cumin
- 1 pinch chili powder
- 1 pinch ground black pepper
- 1 cup shredded Cheddar/Monterey Jack cheese blend
- 2 cups crumbled corn chips

Direction

- In a medium, nonporous glass bowl, mix tequila, ginger, salt, liquid smoke, garlic, lime juice, teriyaki sauce, and water together. Add chicken and turn to coat thoroughly, cover the bowl, and chill in the refrigerator for 2 to 3 hours.
- Meanwhile, thoroughly mix ground black pepper, chili powder, cumin, cayenne pepper, paprika, dill weed, salt, hot pepper sauce, parsley, onion, peppers, tomato, milk, sour cream, and mayonnaise together in a medium bowl until smooth. Cover the bowl, chill until needed.
- Preheat an outdoor grill to medium-high heat and brush oil over the grate lightly, or arrange the oven rack away 6 inches from the heat source and preheat the broiler.
- Remove the chicken from the marinade and discard the remaining marinade. Broil/grill until the chicken is cooked through and the juices are clear, around 3 to 5 minutes per side.
- In a 9 x 13-inch baking dish, arrange the cooked chicken and spread a layer of the dressing on each chicken piece, then add 1/4 cup of cheese blend. Broil until the cheese melts, around 2 to 3 minutes.
- On each of 4 plates, spread a bed of tortilla strips or 1/2 cup of crumbled corn chips. Place a chicken breast on top of each plate to serve.

Nutrition Information

- Calories: 1030 calories;
- Total Fat: 64.9
- Sodium: 2237
- Total Carbohydrate: 68
- Cholesterol: 98
- Protein: 40.8

58. Rompope (Mexican Eggnog)

Serving: 8 | Prep: 10mins | Ready in:

Ingredients

- 3 pints whole milk
- 2 1/2 cups white sugar
- 2 cinnamon sticks
- 15 egg yolks
- 1 cup rum

Direction

- In a big saucepan, mix sugar, cinnamon sticks and milk together then boil over low heat setting. Continue boiling the mixture while stirring continuously for about 20 minutes until a little more than 1/3 of the milk remains. Remove the mixture from the heat and set aside to cool down.
- Using an electric mixer, whisk egg yolks until it is pale in color and thick in consistency. Put in a little amount of the warm milk then mix. Over low heat, boil the egg yolk mixture in a saucepan. Continuously stir the mixture while scraping the sides and bottom of the saucepan as you go for 5 to 7 minutes until it achieves a thick consistency that coats the back of a spoon. Remove the mixture from heat and dispose the cinnamon sticks, let the mixture sit for a while until lukewarm. Mix in rum and let it cool down fully for about 2 hours.

Nutrition Information

- Calories: 516 calories;
- Sodium: 88
- Total Carbohydrate: 72.3
- Cholesterol: 402

- Protein: 10.8
- Total Fat: 14.2

59. Shiner® Bock Shredded Chicken Tacos

Serving: 10 | Prep: 15mins | Ready in:

Ingredients

- 1 whole chicken
- 2 tablespoons chicken fajita seasoning
- 1 tablespoon cayenne pepper
- 2 cups water, or more as needed
- 1 (12 fluid ounce) can or bottle beer (such as Shiner® Bock)
- 1 (16 ounce) can enchilada sauce (such as El Paso® Hot Red Enchilada Sauce)
- 3 fresh jalapeno peppers, diced
- 1 white onion, chopped
- 1 (10 ounce) package corn tortillas, or as needed
- 1 (8 ounce) package shredded Mexican cheese blend, or to taste

Direction

- Place the chicken into a big pot and season with cayenne pepper and fajita seasoning. Pour the beer and water over. Cook the chicken on medium heat until the meat falls from the bone and the center is no longer pink, around 1 hour, add more water if the liquid has reduced too much. An instant-read thermometer should read 74 degrees C or 165 degrees F when inserted in the thickest part of the thigh near the bone. Remove the chicken from the broth mix to a work surface to slightly cool, reserving the broth mix.
- In a big saucepan on a medium-low heat, combine 1/4 cup of the chicken broth mixture with onion, jalapeno peppers, and enchilada sauce; cook until the onions are soft, roughly 10 minutes.
- Take the meat off the chicken and shred into the enchilada sauce mixture, stir well.
- Warm up the tortillas on a grill pan on medium-low heat. Spoon the chicken mixture onto each of the corn tortilla and top with Mexican cheese blend.

Nutrition Information

- Calories: 475 calories;
- Sodium: 434
- Total Carbohydrate: 20
- Cholesterol: 70
- Protein: 19.4
- Total Fat: 34.4

60. Shrimp And Jalapeno Nachos

Serving: 15 | Prep: 20mins | Ready in:

Ingredients

- 1/2 cup sour cream
- 1/2 avocado, peeled and pitted
- 1/2 lemon, juiced
- 1 pound small Gulf shrimp (50 to 60 per pound), thawed and drained
- 1 tablespoon vegetable oil
- 1/4 teaspoon ground dried chipotle pepper
- salt and ground black pepper to taste
- 1 pinch cayenne pepper, or to taste
- 50 large (restaurant-style) tortilla chips, or as needed
- 2 jalapeno peppers, seeded and very thinly sliced
- 3 1/2 cups shredded pepperjack cheese, or as needed
- 15 cherry tomatoes, sliced - or as needed
- 1/4 cup chopped fresh cilantro

Direction

- In a food processor or blender, mix together lemon juice, avocado, and sour cream; process

until creamy and smooth. Remove into a plastic decorating bottle that has a long tip. If necessary, chill the creamy- avocado sauce.
- In a bowl, put shrimp; mix with cayenne pepper, black pepper, salt, ground chipotle pepper, and vegetable oil.
- Heat a big nonstick pan to high heat. In the hot pan, cook shrimp in 1 layer, 1 minute each side, until pink and just cooked through. Remove onto a dish and allow the shrimp to cool.
- Start preheating the oven's broiler. Use an aluminum foil to line a cookie sheet and lightly oil the foil.
- On the prepared cookie sheet, put tortilla chips in 1 layer. Put on each chip with 1 shrimp. Put on a 1 slice jalapeno and top each shrimp with 1 big pinch pepperjack cheese.
- Put under the preheated broiler and broil for 1 minute until the chips have slightly toasted and the cheese has melted. Watch closely as chips will burn quickly.
- Transfer the nachos from the cookie sheet to a serving dish. Before serving, use the avocado-cream sauce to drizzle and cilantro and cherry tomatoes to sprinkle.

Nutrition Information

- Calories: 209 calories;
- Protein: 12.5
- Total Fat: 14.9
- Sodium: 278
- Total Carbohydrate: 6.3
- Cholesterol: 82

61. Shrimp And Octopus Soup (Caldo De Camaron Y Pulpo)

Serving: 8 | Prep: 35mins | Ready in:

Ingredients

- 2 quarts water
- 2 pounds octopus, cut into 1 inch pieces
- 1 tablespoon vegetable oil
- 1 cup diced carrots
- 1 cup diced celery
- 2 cups cubed potatoes
- 1/2 cup crushed dry pasilla chile peppers
- 1/2 cup chopped onion, or to taste
- 1 cup diced tomato
- 1 1/2 pounds large shrimp in shells
- 1 cup fresh corn kernels (optional)
- salt to taste

Direction

- Boil a big soup pot of water over medium-high heat. Add octopus, and keep boiling for about 20 minutes.
- As the octopus boils, in a skillet, heat oil over medium-high heat. Add pasilla pepper, potatoes, celery, and carrots. Fry for about 15 minutes, adding tomato and onion at the very end. You don't need to fully cook the ingredients.
- Once the octopus has boiled for 20 minutes, add the unpeeled shrimps to the octopus, and allow it to boil for another 5 minutes. Add the vegetables from the skillet and use salt to season as you like. If using corn, add to the shrimp. Allow everything to simmer together for 15 minutes.

Nutrition Information

- Calories: 269 calories;
- Total Fat: 5.2
- Sodium: 462
- Total Carbohydrate: 18.4
- Cholesterol: 184
- Protein: 36.4

62. Shrimp, Jicama And Chile Vinegar Salad

Serving: 4 | Prep: 20mins | Ready in:

Ingredients

- 2/3 cup seasoned rice vinegar
- 1/3 cup white sugar
- 2 tablespoons seeded and minced fresh jalapeno pepper, or to taste
- 2 tablespoons chopped fresh cilantro, or more to taste
- 2 cups peeled, shredded jicama
- 1 pound cooked shrimp, shelled and deveined
- 3 tomatillos, husked and sliced
- 3 tomatoes, sliced

Direction

- In a bowl, mix cilantro, jalapeno pepper, sugar, and rice vinegar. Mix until sugar melts.
- In a sealable plastic bag, mix 1/3 of vinegar dressing and jicama. Seal and keep in fridge for an hour.
- Put shrimp in another sealable plastic bag with 1/3 of dressing. Seal then keep in fridge for an hour. Keep leftover vinegar dressing in the fridge.
- Put alternative slices of tomato and tomatillo around the salad plate edges.
- Mount the marinated jicama in the middle of the plate and put marinated shrimp on top.
- Place leftover 1/3 of dressing on salad.

Nutrition Information

- Calories: 260 calories;
- Sodium: 1104
- Total Carbohydrate: 35.8
- Cholesterol: 221
- Protein: 25.3
- Total Fat: 1.7

63. Simple Shrimp Tostadas

Serving: 6 | Prep: 20mins | Ready in:

Ingredients

- 2 tomatoes, finely chopped
- 1 bunch fresh cilantro, finely chopped
- 1 small red onion, finely chopped (optional)
- 6 tablespoons mayonnaise
- 6 crispy tostada shells
- 1 pound frozen cooked shrimp, thawed
- 2 avocados, thinly sliced
- salt and ground black pepper to taste

Direction

- In a bowl, mix together red onion, cilantro, and tomatoes.
- Spread onto each tostada with one tablespoon of the mayonnaise. Add 2-3 tablespoons of the tomato mixture on top. Place an even layer of the shrimp onto each tostada. Place avocado slices on top; season with pepper and salt.

Nutrition Information

- Calories: 345 calories;
- Total Fat: 24.1
- Sodium: 304
- Total Carbohydrate: 15.9
- Cholesterol: 153
- Protein: 18.6

64. Slow Cooker Cilantro Lime Chicken

Serving: 6 | Prep: 10mins | Ready in:

Ingredients

- 1 (16 ounce) jar salsa
- 1 (1.25 ounce) package dry taco seasoning mix
- 1 lime, juiced
- 3 tablespoons chopped fresh cilantro
- 3 pounds skinless, boneless chicken breast halves

Direction

- In a slow cooker, put the cilantro, lime juice, taco seasoning and salsa, then mix to blend. Put in chicken breasts, then mix to coat with salsa mix. Cover the cooker, set to High, then cook for 4 hours until the chicken is very soft. Set the cooker to Low and cook for 6 to 8 hours, if you like. Shred chicken using 2 forks, serve.

Nutrition Information

- Calories: 272 calories;
- Total Fat: 4.7
- Sodium: 976
- Total Carbohydrate: 9.3
- Cholesterol: 117
- Protein: 45.3

65. Slow Cooker Spicy Chicken

Serving: 3 | Prep: 15mins | Ready in:

Ingredients

- 3 skinless, boneless chicken breast halves
- 1/2 (8 ounce) jar medium salsa
- 1/4 cup tomato sauce
- 2 cloves garlic, minced
- 1 small red onion, chopped
- 1 teaspoon ground cumin
- 1 teaspoon chili powder
- 1 pinch salt and fresh ground pepper to taste

Direction

- In the bottom of a slow cooker, place the chicken breast; add tomato sauce and salsa. Put in pepper, garlic, salt, onion, cumin, and chili powder. Cook chicken for 4-5 hours in a cooker set on Low. Use 2 forks to shred chicken. Serve.

Nutrition Information

- Calories: 152 calories;
- Protein: 24.4
- Total Fat: 2.8
- Sodium: 392
- Total Carbohydrate: 7.1
- Cholesterol: 61

66. Southwest Corn Chowder

Serving: 12 | Prep: 35mins | Ready in:

Ingredients

- 1 pound tomatillos, husked
- 2 tablespoons butter
- 1 onion, diced
- 1 (20 ounce) can white hominy, drained
- 1 teaspoon chopped fresh marjoram
- 1 teaspoon fresh thyme leaves
- 4 cups milk
- 4 sprigs parsley
- 6 ears fresh corn kernels
- 2 roasted red peppers, drained and chopped
- 2 tablespoons chopped fresh cilantro

Direction

- Set a large soup pot filled with water over high heat and bring to a boil. Add in tomatillos; return to a boil for 10 minutes, then drain.
- Meanwhile, in a large saucepan set over medium heat, melt butter. Cook the onions for 5 minutes or until they turn clear and tender. Add thyme, hominy, and marjoram; cook and stir for 5 more minutes. Mix in half of the corn kernels, milk, and parsley; allow the mixture to simmer over medium-high heat.
- In a food processor or blender, add the remaining corn and tomatillos and puree. Add to the soup and mix in the roasted peppers. Leave the soup to simmer for 10 minutes; take out the parsley sprigs. Garnish with cilantro before serving.

Nutrition Information

- Calories: 177 calories;
- Cholesterol: 12
- Protein: 6.7
- Total Fat: 5.3
- Sodium: 218
- Total Carbohydrate: 28.7

67. Southwestern Chicken Pitas With Chipotle Sauce

Serving: 4 | Prep: 30mins | Ready in:

Ingredients

- 1 cup plain nonfat yogurt
- 4 tablespoons chopped green onions
- 2 chipotle peppers
- 4 tablespoons peanut butter
- 1/4 teaspoon salt
- 1 pound skinless, boneless chicken breast halves - cut into 1/2 inch strips
- 1/2 teaspoon salt
- 1/2 teaspoon pepper
- 1/2 teaspoon chili powder
- 1/2 teaspoon garlic powder
- 1/2 teaspoon dried oregano
- 1/2 teaspoon ground cumin
- 3 tablespoons vegetable oil, divided
- 1 medium onion, sliced
- 1 red bell pepper, julienned
- 4 (6-inch) pitas
- 1 cup shredded lettuce
- 1 cup shredded white Cheddar cheese

Direction

- Process the 1/4 teaspoon salt, peanut butter, chipotle peppers, chopped green onion and yogurt in a food processor or blender until it becomes smooth. Transfer in a sealed container then chill in the fridge.
- Set an oven to preheat at 175°C (350°F).
- In a big bowl, put the chicken. Mix the cumin, oregano, chili powder, pepper and 1/2 teaspoon salt together, then sprinkle it on the chicken. In a pan, heat 1/2 of the oil on medium heat. Sauté red peppers and onions until it becomes soft, then move to a plate and put aside. Use foil to wrap the pitas and put it in the oven for about 10 minutes.
- In a pan, heat the leftover oil, then sauté the chicken until not pink anymore. Put red peppers and onions and cook for an additional 2 minutes.
- Halve the pitas and stuff it with the chicken mixture. Serve alongside chipotle sauce, cheese and lettuce.

Nutrition Information

- Calories: 647 calories;
- Total Carbohydrate: 48.2
- Cholesterol: 97
- Protein: 46.3
- Total Fat: 30.3
- Sodium: 1155

68. Spicy Cheesy Refried Beans

Serving: 6 | Prep: 10mins | Ready in:

Ingredients

- 1 tablespoon butter
- 1/4 cup chopped onion
- 1 tablespoon chopped garlic
- 1 (16 ounce) can spicy fat-free refried beans
- 1 (4 ounce) package cream cheese
- 1 cup shredded Cheddar cheese

Direction

- Preheat an oven to 175 °C or 350 °F.
- In a saucepan, melt butter over medium heat; cook and mix the garlic and onion for 2 to 3 minutes till onion turns translucent.

- Into the onion mixture, cook and mix refried beans for 3 to 5 minutes till warmed heated. Take off heat and into bean mixture, mix the cream cheese. Into a pie plate, scatter the mixture; put Cheddar cheese on top.
- In the prepped oven, bake for 20 minutes till cheese is bubbling and melted.

Nutrition Information

- Calories: 224 calories;
- Protein: 10
- Total Fat: 14.7
- Sodium: 541
- Total Carbohydrate: 12.8
- Cholesterol: 46

69. Sylvia's Pork Tamales

Serving: 36 | Prep: 1hours | Ready in:

Ingredients

- 3 pounds pork butt roast
- 1 large onion, chopped
- 5 cloves garlic
- 1 tablespoon salt
- water to cover
- 3 ounces California chile pods, seeds and veins removed
- 3 ounces New Mexico chile pods, seeds and veins removed
- 1 cup pork broth
- 1 cup water
- 1 tablespoon salt
- 3 cloves garlic
- 1 teaspoon ground cumin
- 1/2 cup lard
- 1/2 cup all-purpose flour
- salt to taste
- 1 (8 ounce) package dried corn husks
- 5 pounds masa harina
- 1 pound lard
- 1 tablespoon baking powder

Direction

- In a large pot, put one tablespoon of salt, 5 cloves garlic, onion and pork butt; add water to cover. Over medium heat, simmer the mixture for 3 hours or until the pork becomes very tender. Remove garlic and onion. Strain, then shred the meat, saving liquid.
- Over medium-high heat, heat a skillet. In hot skillet, cook while stirring New Mexico chile pods and California chile pods for 2 to 3 mins or until fragrant and toasted. Rinse the chile pods. Boil water in a pot and put in the chile pods; boil for 3 mins or until the chile pods are softened slightly. Drain. Allow chile pods to cool.
- In a blender, blend together cumin, 3 cloves garlic, one tablespoon of salt, chile pods, one cup of water and one cup of the pork broth until they become smooth. In a bowl, stir together chile sauce and pork meat.
- Melt 1/2 cup lard in a large pot over medium heat. Stir flour into melted lard until browned and fragrant, about 5 mins. Stir pork-chile sauce mixture into flour mixture, adding more salt if needed.
- Discard debris and silk from the corn husks. Then soak for 30-60 minutes in the boiling water. Drain, then put on the work surface; wrap in the clean, damp towel.
- In a large pan, mix salt, baking powder, one cup of the reserved pork broth, 1 pound lard and masa until the mixture holds together and becomes fluffy.
- Take two small corn husks or 1 wide one. Spread over corn husk with 2 tablespoons of masa mixture, spreading 2-in. from bottom and 1/4-in. from top and to the sides. Spoon down middle of the masa mixture with 1 to 2 tablespoons of the pork mixture. Fold together sides of the husk, one over the other. Then fold the husk bottom over seam of the two folded sides. Do the same with the remaining filling and husks.
- In a saucepan, put a steamer insert and pour in water to just below bottom of steamer. Bring water to a boil. Put in tamales. Cook for 1 to 2

hours or until the filling is set and heated through. Allow tamales to rest for half an hour. Then serve.

Nutrition Information

- Calories: 436 calories;
- Cholesterol: 30
- Protein: 10.3
- Total Fat: 21.6
- Sodium: 449
- Total Carbohydrate: 52

70. Taco Slaw

Serving: 6 | Prep: 20mins | Ready in:

Ingredients

- 1/2 small head cabbage, chopped
- 1 jalapeno pepper, seeded and minced
- 1/2 red onion, minced
- 1 carrot, chopped
- 1 tablespoon chopped fresh cilantro
- 1 lime, juiced

Direction

- Combine carrot, lime juice, cabbage, red onion, cilantro, and jalapeno pepper in a bowl.

Nutrition Information

- Calories: 27 calories;
- Sodium: 19
- Total Carbohydrate: 6.6
- Cholesterol: 0
- Protein: 1.1
- Total Fat: 0.1

71. Tongue Tacos

Serving: 6 | Prep: 20mins | Ready in:

Ingredients

- 1 beef tongue
- 2 tomatoes, diced
- 1 onion, diced
- 1 bunch fresh cilantro, chopped
- 1 tablespoon vegetable oil
- salt and pepper to taste
- 6 (6 inch) corn tortillas
- 3 tablespoons lemon juice

Direction

- Add enough water to cover the tongue and simmer till not pink anymore, approximately 50 minutes for each pound of tongue. Take off from water and allow to sit till cool enough to touch. Remove the tongue skin, trim off the gristle, and slice into small-size portions.
- Meanwhile, in medium bowl, mix cilantro, onion and tomatoes. Combine thoroughly and put aside.
- Heat the oil in big skillet over moderate heat. Let tongue cook with pepper and salt for 5 to 10 minutes till heated completely and partially colored. Allow to drain.
- Heat the tortillas in a small skillet, for a minute per side. To put tacos together, in one folded tortilla, pile tongue and tomato mixture and drizzle with juice of lemon. Serve right away.

Nutrition Information

- Calories: 566 calories;
- Sodium: 126
- Total Carbohydrate: 15.9
- Cholesterol: 218
- Protein: 34.2
- Total Fat: 40.1

72. Traditional Mexican Guacamole

Serving: 4 | Prep: 10mins | Ready in:

Ingredients

- 2 avocados, peeled and pitted
- 1 cup chopped tomatoes
- 1/4 cup chopped onion
- 1/4 cup chopped cilantro
- 2 tablespoons lemon juice
- 1 jalapeno pepper, seeded and minced (optional)
- salt and ground black pepper to taste

Direction

- Prepare a bowl then put avocados in it and crush them until becomes creamy.
- Add in the jalapeno pepper, lemon juice, cilantro, onion and tomatoes then mix well; add black pepper and salt to taste.

Nutrition Information

- Calories: 176 calories;
- Sodium: 50
- Total Carbohydrate: 12.2
- Cholesterol: 0
- Protein: 2.7
- Total Fat: 14.9

73. Traditional Mexican Street Tacos

Serving: 2 | Prep: 10mins | Ready in:

Ingredients

- 6 (5 inch) corn tortillas
- 3 cups chopped cooked chicken
- 4 sprigs fresh cilantro, chopped
- 1/2 cup chopped white onion
- 1 cup guacamole
- 1 lime, cut into wedges

Direction

- Line a microwave-safe plate with a paper towel and put the tortillas on top; heat in the microwave for 10 seconds.
- Place the chicken in a microwavable bowl; heat in the microwave for 30 seconds to 1 minute until heated through.
- In this order - chicken, cilantro, onion, and guacamole layer each tortilla. Sprinkle lime juice on top of each taco.

Nutrition Information

- Calories: 697 calories;
- Sodium: 177
- Total Carbohydrate: 44.2
- Cholesterol: 158
- Protein: 64.1
- Total Fat: 29.9

74. Vegan Mexican Quinoa Bowl With Green Chile Cilantro Sauce

Serving: 4 | Prep: 30mins | Ready in:

Ingredients

- Vegan Green Chile Cilantro Sauce:
- 1 cup unsalted raw cashews
- 1 (4 ounce) can chopped green chile peppers
- 1/4 cup hemp milk
- 1/2 jalapeno pepper with seeds, or more to taste
- 1/2 teaspoon salt
- 1 1/4 cups chopped fresh cilantro
- 3 cups water
- 1 1/2 cups quinoa
- 2 romaine hearts, chopped
- 2 (15 ounce) cans black beans, rinsed and drained
- 3 cups chopped red bell pepper

- 1/2 cup chopped red onion
- 2 avocados, chopped

Direction

- Process salt, jalapeno pepper, hemp milk, green chile peppers and cashews till smooth in a blender.
- Put cashew mixture into small bowl; mix in 1 cup of cilantro.
- Boil quinoa and water in a saucepan. Lower heat to medium low and cover; simmer for 15-20 minutes till quinoa is tender.
- Divide romaine lettuce to 4 bowls; top with onion, red bell pepper, black beans and quinoa. Drizzle cilantro sauce; garnish with chopped avocados and leftover 1/4 cup cilantro.

Nutrition Information

- Calories: 694 calories;
- Total Carbohydrate: 101.5
- Cholesterol: 0
- Protein: 31.3
- Total Fat: 20.5
- Sodium: 1476

75. Vegetarian Tortilla Soup With Avocado

Serving: 8 | Prep: 20mins | Ready in:

Ingredients

- 3 flour tortillas, cut into strips
- cooking spray
- 1 tablespoon peanut oil, or as needed
- 1 1/2 cups chopped onion
- 1/4 cup chopped red bell peppers
- 2 cloves garlic, minced
- 1 (14.5 ounce) can stewed tomatoes with juice, chopped
- 2 cups diced zucchini
- 2 cups frozen sweet corn
- 1/2 cup diced mushrooms
- 5 cups vegetable broth
- 3/4 tablespoon chili powder
- 1 1/2 teaspoons hot pepper sauce
- salt and ground black pepper to taste
- 2 tablespoons chopped fresh cilantro
- 1 avocado - peeled, pitted, and sliced
- 1 cup shredded Monterey Jack cheese

Direction

- Preheat oven to 375°F (190°C).
- On a baking sheet, pile tortilla chips and lightly coat with cooking spray. Place inside the preheated oven and bake for 8-10 minutes until crispy and golden in color.
- Place a stockpot on the stove and turn on to medium-high heat then put peanut oil. Sauté garlic, red bell pepper and onion for 5-10 minutes until onion turns translucent. Stir in mushrooms, corn, zucchini and tomatoes with juice; fry for 3 to 4 minutes until zucchini is slightly softened.
- Add into vegetable mixture the pepper, salt, hot sauce, chili powder and vegetable broth; bring to boil. Lower heat and gently boil soup for 20-25 minutes until vegetables are tender. Mix cilantro into soup and remove stockpot from heat.
- Place soup into serving bowls; put Monterey Jack cheese, avocado slices and tortilla chips on top.

Nutrition Information

- Calories: 259 calories;
- Sodium: 621
- Total Carbohydrate: 32.2
- Cholesterol: 13
- Protein: 8.9
- Total Fat: 12

Index

A
Avocado 3,41

B
Banana 3,26
Beans 3,6,37
Beef 3,7
Beer 3,8
Bread 3,22
Burger 3,9
Butter 3,26

C
Cheddar 3,6,7,8,9,11,12,18,19,29,32,37,38
Cheese 3,16,25,26
Chicken 3,8,9,10,11,12,15,16,21,24,27,29,31,33,35,36,37
Chipotle 3,37
Chorizo 3,18
Coconut 3,11
Cream 3,5,16

D
Dijon mustard 20

E
Egg 3,32

F
Fat 4,5,6,7,8,9,10,11,12,13,14,15,16,17,18,19,20,21,22,23,24,25,26,27,28,29,30,31,32,33,34,35,36,37,38,39,40,41
Flank 3,20

G
Flour 8
Fruit 3,14

G
Guacamole 3,9,13,26,40

H
Hominy 3,21
Honey 8

J
Jam 9

L
Lemon 3,25
Lime 3,17,31,35

M
Mango 3,17
Meat 4,22

N
Nachos 3,16,33
Nut 4,5,6,7,8,9,10,11,12,13,14,15,16,17,18,19,20,21,22,23,24,25,26,27,28,29,30,31,32,33,34,35,36,37,38,39,40,41

O
Octopus 3,34
Oil 4

P
Parmesan 13
Pear 3,28
Pepper 3,29,31
Pie 3,27
Pineapple 3,9
Pizza 3,18
Pork 3,18,38

Q

Quinoa 3,5,24,40

R

Rice 3,6,24

S

Salad 3,5,15,17,34

Salsa 3,4,6,14,30

Sausage 8,18

Shin 3,33

Soup 3,12,15,25,26,31,34,41

Steak 3,20

Sugar 8

Syrup 8

T

Taco 3,4,6,8,10,24,26,27,29,33,39,40

Tequila 3,31

Tomato 3,14

Tongue 3,39

V

Vegan 3,40

Vegetarian 3,41

Vinegar 3,34

W

Worcestershire sauce 20

Y

Yeast 4

Conclusion

Thank you again for downloading this book!

I hope you enjoyed reading about my book!

If you enjoyed this book, please take the time to share your thoughts and post a review on Amazon. It'd be greatly appreciated!

Write me an honest review about the book – I truly value your opinion and thoughts and I will incorporate them into my next book, which is already underway.

Thank you!

If you have any questions, **feel free to contact at:** *author@bunrecipes.com*

Paula Lopez

bunrecipes.com

Made in United States
Orlando, FL
21 July 2022